'Owen was a childhood phenom who grew into the ultimate family man. In between this transition, he took on the world, charged crazy waves, suffered a huge brain injury, and finished off with the all-time sporting comeback! Surrounded by family and friends, his life has been the ultimate roller coaster.'
Mick Fanning, three-time world champion surfer

'Owen is one those guys that I believe operates on one speed. It's the "let's fucking go" speed. Sunday BBQ? Let's fucking go. Fifteen-foot barrels onto dry reef? Let's fucking go. Whatever it is that Owen is getting himself into, he seems to do it with little to no fear and a massive smile on his face. His infectious humour and laughter is something you'll never get tired of. He's an inspirational guy, to put it lightly. Owen is one special human!'
Liam Hemsworth, actor

'Owen Wright has to be the most inspiring person I've ever met. I'm not only saying this with bias as his wife, but because I have never seen anyone with as much resilience, determination and natural talent as him. His story is one of a childhood prodigy, to facing a near-death experience, to Australian hero . . . This book will inspire and motivate anyone who has had to face adversity whilst following their dreams.'
Kita Alexander, singer-songwriter

'In the middle of the lockdowns, Owen came to stay with us. He had the North American leg of surf tour season and the Olympics right around the corner. Owen's work ethic was apparent right from the get-go. All the gyms were closed, so Ow went to Walmart and brought home a $50 stationary bike. It was so small and so cheap but, let me tell you, that little bike could go. He would crush ten miles every day, never missing a beat. The mental capacity it took to do that many miles on that small of a bike . . . That's a true fighter's spirit! He never once got distracted or made an excuse in a time when everybody was, including myself. So obviously, when he took the bronze at the Olympics, I wasn't surprised. I took that little Walmart bike and powder coated it bronze. She still sits in my front yard today, like a beautiful little lawn ornament. In memory of Ow and the Olympic dream.'

Luke Rockhold, UFC middleweight champion, two-time jiu-jitsu world champion, three-time strikeforce middleweight champion

AGAINST THE WATER

AGAINST THE WATER

OWEN WRIGHT

**A surfing champion's inspirational journey
to Olympic glory**

SIMON &
SCHUSTER

London · New York · Sydney · Toronto · New Delhi

AGAINST THE WATER: A SURFING CHAMPION'S INSPIRATIONAL
JOURNEY TO OLYMPIC GLORY
First published in Australia in 2023 by
Simon & Schuster (Australia) Pty Limited
Suite 19A, Level 1, Building C, 450 Miller Street, Cammeray, NSW 2062

10 9 8 7 6 5 4 3 2 1

Sydney New York London Toronto New Delhi
Visit our website at www.simonandschuster.com.au

A catalogue record for this
book is available from the
National Library of Australia

ISBN: 9781761106576

Photographs in the photo insert used with kind permission of the author.

Cover design by Meng Koach
Cover image by Lawrence Furzey
Typeset by Midland Typesetters, Australia
Printed and bound in Australia by Griffin Press

The paper this book is printed on is certified against the
Forest Stewardship Council® Standards. Griffin Press holds
chain of custody certification SCS-COC-001185. FSC®
promotes environmentally responsible, socially beneficial
and economically viable management of the world's forests.

Dedicated to:
Mum and Dad. My wife Kita
and our beautiful children.

CONTENTS

'Long is the way and hard, that out of hell leads up to light.'
– Milton

PROLOGUE

SUNLIGHT STRIKES MY EYES, coaxing me awake. I'm curled up in a hotel bed in Chiba, east of Tokyo. Shortly, I'll be surfing for an Olympic medal, but my waking thought is that it's 27 July – my mother's birthday. Should I call her now? No, I'll wait. First, I'll compete, because if I can make that call as an Olympic champion, it would be some gift; it would trump, 'Hi, Mum, happy birthday – what have you got planned?'

It's 5.05 am. I tossed and turned most of the night. But sleep and I are done with each other. I shift onto my back and close my eyes, blocking out everything except the sensation of my breathing. I want to feel so calm and ethereal that I could float out the door.

I decide to do this visualisation thing that I'm into. What I do is take myself back to an event where I surfed well. Specifically, I time-travel to March 2017 at Snapper Rocks, when I returned to the tour after getting hurt in Hawaii. I'll tell you all about Hawaii later, but the short version is I suffered a brain injury at Banzai Pipeline that almost killed me. On my road back, Snapper Rocks was monumental for me. Now, I spend five minutes basking in the memory, including being held aloft by my sister Tyler and my brother Mikey in the moments after I'd won. They're standing knee-deep in the

1

ocean – I can see Mikey's savage mullet from above – with me hoisted on their shoulders and people all around us. My left arm is thrust skywards, and I'm feeling a sense of jubilation tinged with disbelief.

Then I take a trip into the future. I'm at home in Lennox Head on the New South Wales North Coast with my family – my wife, Kita, my little boy, Vali and my baby girl, Rumi. Around my neck hangs an Olympic medal. I muse on that for a few minutes.

I reach for my phone. It bothers me that I'm feeling weary rather than primed. I refuse to carry negative thoughts into the surf. It's something I know all about – I can tell you that it's death to good surfing. I fire off a text to the surf team's psychologist and we arrange to meet in the lobby.

Jason Patchell and I have been working together for five years. Our relationship has endured because he's a gem of a guy who's terrific at what he does. When he switches from regular Jason to psychologist Jason, there's a shift in his tone that says you're now his sole focus – you're the only person in the world he cares about right now. The tone is kind and soothing, like a mother's hug.

I've already leaned on Jason more than once this year in states near to despair. Although I qualified for the Olympics as Australia's second-highest-ranked male surfer, I came here on a losing streak. While my surfing was passable and slowly improving, I couldn't win a heat to save myself. You know how it is when things you could once do effortlessly are now chal-lenging, if not impossible? That's where I was with my surfing. My ranking was based on 2019 results, which would have been superseded except the pandemic wiped out the 2020 World Surf League (WSL) tour.

As the Games neared, I was climbing the walls. This would be surfing's first appearance at the Olympics, and I'd be competing in front of the largest television audience in the sport's history. I had every reason to be pessimistic, yet now I'm here, things have somehow clicked. It's as though my expectations have sunk to the ocean floor, taking most of my agitation along with them.

I've already beaten several class acts, and as I've racked up the wins, my confidence has soared. Now, entering this final day, surfing no longer seems like a physical and mental exam, but rather something I was born to do – precisely the right delusion to take into competition.

There's just this problem of a wretched night's sleep.

At the hotel's main door, Jason and I take in the rain hammering the pavement and a howling wind bending the trees – typhoon Nepartek is venting its fury. In better weather, a stroll in the dawn light would be ideal. But we settle for the comfort of a hotel couch.

'Mate, you're at the Olympics. Broken sleep is part of the ride,' Jason says. 'You don't feel as bright-eyed as you'd like to? Well, acknowledge that and move on. Do what you need to do.'

Right, I think. And now, what I need to do are these exercises that I've routinised since the disaster at Pipe. Really, they're less exercises than basic movements such as crawling, rolling over and pushing myself off the floor with my hands – moves a baby learns to do naturally. They're the tools of a rehabilitation technique called Dynamic Neuromuscular Stabilisation, which has been part of my recovery. This morning, the WSL's medical director, Chris Prosser, guides me through a circuit. Afterwards, as usual, I feel more in tune with my body, more capable of performing athletically.

Time to fuel up. On non-competition days, my breakfast is three eggs. Before a heat, though, I'll have muesli, and the more nervous I am, the less I'll eat. Today, I manage three mouthfuls.

COME MIDMORNING ON TSURIGASKA BEACH, the weather has turned wilder. The wind blowing from the north reminds me of the cyclonic conditions we get back home on the New South Wales North Coast. The rain is coming down sideways, and it's cold – I need a jacket and long pants to ward off the chills.

The surf is the biggest I've seen here – big and messy. We're going to be paddling out in a washing machine. Am I worried? Not at all. Although I've had my ups and downs with big waves (to say the least), I relish these conditions because when the surf's angry like this, you're in mother nature's hands; you either work with her or you flounder. To score well, you need a particular set of ocean skills, which I know I have. I've always preferred a churning mess to lake-like conditions, where the task becomes trying to milk something out of nothing. Some guys excel at this. I don't.

My opponent is Ítalo Ferreira, of Brazil. Ferreira's a nuggety customer, 168 centimetres tall – a completely different body shape to mine. I'm a rangy 193 centimetres tall. Ferreira rocks some of the flashiest hairstyles on the tour and has the moves to match. I reckon he would have been hoping for small waves, because it's on these he does some of his sharpest work and he knows they don't suit me. As things stand, Ferreira, who was the 2019 world champion, would outperform me over the course of a year. But on a given day, mano a mano in gnarly surf, I'm a fighting chance.

Out we go, with 30 minutes to show our wares. In pro surfing, your final score is the aggregate of your two highest-scoring waves, as determined by a five-person judging panel. My lack of sleep is forgotten. I'm ready.

Ferreira enters a wave-catching frenzy. His strategy is to grab as many as possible with the aim of jagging at least a couple of solid returns early and forcing me to play catch-up. Mostly, he's getting piddling scores in the 2s and 3s (out of 10), but he does pull off a whopping aerial to earn a 6.67, which combines with another 6+ wave to ensure he'll post a competitive score.

In the chop, I take a couple of falls before finding my rhythm. Like Ferreira, I record two 6+ scores, but as the clock is winding down, I'm losing. I resist the urge to rush or press, and not for a second do I count myself out, but try as I might, I can't muster a heat-stealing ride. The scoreboard flashes its grim verdict:

Ferreira: 13.17
Wright: 12.47

It's Ferreira who'll be surfing for the gold medal; my next date will be the battle for bronze.

I'm met back on the sand by my teammate, Julian Wilson (Jules).

'Devo,' I say.

'Yeah, it looked like you were just trying too hard,' Jules says.

Now, that's a line surfers use a lot. As a gesture of commiseration, it's standard. But I'm not ready to hear any feedback. And I'm not sure Jules' feedback is fair. I know he's referring to those falls I took; he's implying I made mistakes out there. But had I?

Australia's head coach, Bede Durbidge, and Jason the psychologist join me. The bronze-medal heat is only about an hour away, so Bede and Jason want me to let go of this defeat and zero in on the next task. But I can't do that yet. Though innocently meant, Jules' comment has unsettled me.

'I need to see the footage,' I tell Bede, who's filmed the heat. 'I can't move on until I've had a look.'

Bede fiddles with his camera, fast-forwarding to the waves in question. The three of us stand there on the beach in the rain and wind, huddled over the backscreen. I need to know, did I really *try too hard* or was I simply undone by wild surf? This is not about ego or self-flagellation; it's about settling on the right approach to my next heat. Should I go out there with the same pressure on the accelerator, or ease back?

I watch the footage with a racing heart. I see myself on the lip of the first wave. I've done everything right, but the wave is so unruly that it spits me out like a lump of gristle. I watch the second wave. I see myself doing exactly what I should have done in the wind and chop, which is to be conservative and turn *under* the lip, but again this wave is an amorphous brute that drops me like a bad habit.

I did okay, I realise. In terms of mentality – bold but sensible – I got it right. And I should, I resolve, surf the same way when I head back out. In my mind, the loss to Ferreira and Jules' comment are history.

'Thanks,' I say. 'Shut the camera.'

'Great,' says Jason. 'Put a line through it. We're moving forward.'

THERE'S A MEDAL TO be won. Suddenly, that is the only thing that matters; its colour is immaterial. My opponent will be another Brazilian, Gabriel Medina. Almost four years younger than me, this guy's a two-time world champion who's in absurdly good form. While winning was a memory for me when I landed in Japan, Medina's been cleaning up wherever he goes. Besides Kelly Slater, he's also the fiercest and most cunning competitor in boardshorts. In this contest, I'm the gigantic underdog.

Medina and I have a backstory. After he won the Rip Curl Search in San Francisco in 2011 at the age of seventeen, I joined the celebration that night with a bunch of boisterous Brazilians. Although I couldn't understand much of what they were saying, I wanted to be there as a show of respect to a fellow competitor and champion in the making. At one point, late in the night, Gaby turned to me.

'Owen?'

'Hey, mate.'

'You won't remember this, but when I was twelve there was a junior world title event near Maresias Beach in São Sebastião where I grew up. You were competing and you broke your board in the surf.'

'Yeah, that's right,' I said. 'How do you remember that?'

'I fetched half the board from the water and gave it back to you.'

'Wow! That was you? Thank you.'

For me, it's a piece of history that's still nice to think about. I'm sure it helped bond us. Outside of the tour, Medina and I check in on each other and catch up when we can. He's great with Vali. He knows how to make the little fellow laugh, and guys who can make kids laugh are nearly always nice guys.

Medina *is* a good guy. But this isn't tiddlywinks, and like I told you, he plays to win. Which I'm about to be reminded of.

When Bede and I enter the change room, Medina is sitting with his coach right underneath my locker. Believe me, this is no absentminded mistake. They know exactly what they're doing: invading our space, daring us to respond. Pure gamesmanship. Bede and I have three options. We can move over to the other side of the room where *they* should be; we can tell them to fuck off; or we can hold our ground. Wordlessly, we settle on option three.

I stand next to Medina and start getting changed. I'm towering over him because I'm quite a bit taller. Bede gets in on the caper, too, talking louder than usual – and deeper unless I'm mistaken. To you, this might all sound a bit juvenile, but what's really going on is that Medina is letting me know that our friendship is out the window – suspended, at least – for the next hour or so. And you know what? I like this little macho head game he's initiated. It's putting me in a headspace where all I want to do is get out there and compete like the devil and absolutely flog these guys.

I leave the change room and jog up the stairs to the pavilion's first floor, from where I can get a clearer idea of the conditions. Surfers will do this whenever we can, especially when the ocean's wild. At ground level, all you can see is whitewash, but from higher ground, you can identify where the waves are breaking and the pockets to put yourself in. While I'm up here, I hop on a stationary bike and roll my legs over.

The truth is, I'm feeling the pressure like a rhino on my back. There's no escaping that I'm the surf team's last hope to bring something home from Japan more tangible than memories. On the women's side, Sally Fitzgibbons had been among the favourites until a local charger, Amuro Tsuzuki, stunned her in the quarterfinals. It feels like yesterday that Sal and I were a pair of big-dreaming grommets from the New South Wales South Coast, who surfed together as teenagers and became mates. When she dissolved into tears after losing and told reporters, 'It hurts so bad,' I knew everything I needed to know about how I'd be feeling if I left here empty-handed.

Why are my nerves so intense? And is it just nerves or something else: fear? Not of physical harm but of losing? Previously, I coped with anxiety at events by telling myself that this is all about me – my ambition, my opportunities, my self-respect – and that very few people care whether I win or lose. But that won't work this time. It feels like all the giants of Australian surfing, past and present, are watching, willing me to prevail.

Perched here on this bike, I accept my fate. Onto my shoulders has fallen a task, the outcome of which matters. And these, surely, are the moments we live for – to have something mean so much that you're freaking out. *Feel the fear*, I tell myself. *Stare the Olympic beast in the face. Stare it down.* Stare it down now, and then, once you're out there, forget it. Fall back on the knowledge that you've been surfing for twenty-five years.

I have these words that I say to myself before I compete: I trust in my best. And another phrase: connected warrior. That means being connected to the ocean, to my feelings, to the moment, but not helplessly – actively. Yes, I'm in tune with the universe, if you like, but I'm also a warrior. And a ferocious one.

SHOW TIME. THE ANNOUNCER introduces me. Although the wind is still gusting, the sun has peeked out from behind dark clouds. By now, I'm in a serious mood, maybe too serious. As well as being a warrior, I like to carry a sense of joy into competition. So, I use my right hand to simulate the action of a jellyfish's sting. The Australian surf team has recently acquired a new moniker: we're the Irukandjis, named after the lethal species of jellyfish in the waters off northern Australia. We like to think we're 'Deadly in the Water' – this team claim makes us smile and, in my case, hopefully relax.

As I'm running up the beach towards my preferred entry point, I sense someone beside me. What on earth? More mind games from Medina? No, it's Jules.

'You've got this, man,' he says. 'Let's go.'

I figure he'll peel off then, but I'm wrong. He keeps running right alongside me. It's unusual, but I can't tell you how much I love it. I've known Jules since I was ten. We've surfed as mates, as competitors, and we've travelled the world together. Him being at my shoulder now makes me feel like my team is carrying me in loving arms.

Medina and I paddle out and begin jockeying for position. I know what his tactics will be. Like Ferreira, he's going to shoot for quantity: lots of waves, crappy or otherwise, because he has this ability to do aerials, or airs, off dismal offerings.

My first couple are okay, nothing amazing, each yielding about 5 points. Suddenly, the ocean smooths and I'm well positioned to catch this clean-faced right-hander, on which I execute three strong turns. *Oh, yeah.* That felt solid. That felt like an opportunity seized. I score 6.5, the best so far for either of us with half the heat gone. *One more of those*, I think.

Time is flying. I'm switched on, spotting and assessing every bump in the ocean. At the same time, I'm not giving Medina any room. I don't want him to have any sense of free rein, any sense that he can take his sweet time to express his talent. For now, he's getting half-chances but falling.

The waves are getting worse – more unruly – until out of nowhere, a promising set looms. I shift about, judge the first wave as too big, too foamy, before jumping on the second. I'm up and going, and manage a frontside snap in the crest of the wave, which shifts me sideways before it dips and re-peaks, allowing me to execute another big turn before it peters out.

All right. That's my back-up wave. I'm in the game with enough time still to get another one.

Except this last wave has deposited me way left of the comp zone, with a barrage of whitewash blocking my way back to where Medina is now operating unchecked. I could leave the water, dash up the beach and re-enter the surf rather than paddling out and across, but either way it's going to be a slog.

I'm weary, but so what? If this isn't a time to empty your reserves, then when is? I stay in the water and paddle back, which takes about thirty duck dives and most of the gas I have left. But the point is, I'm back in Medina's face and time is running out for him. He has one decent wave in the bag – a 6.0 – but he'll need another one to beat me. More than likely, he'll need an air, because the quality of wave is still deteriorating.

For me, it's time to switch to smothering tactics. Because he's caught the last wave, I have priority for the next one. That means I have the unconditional right of way to catch any wave I choose. And while Medina's allowed to paddle for, and catch, the same wave, he can't obstruct me or hinder my scoring potential. So, I sit close to him, evaluating every wave but not pulling the trigger. He ends up choosing a wave that's terrible and falls attempting an air. Worse for him, he gets stuck on the inside for four precious minutes. By the time he busts through the break, there's only ninety seconds to go.

I'm way out the back in the best place to catch a wave, yet I know it's not where I need to be. Fear is rising – fear that Medina will catch something unimpeded and win. So, I heed my fear, which tells me unequivocally what to do: switch off my wave-catching instincts and get my butt in closer to shore – closer to Medina.

Sure enough, with twenty seconds left, this clean-faced right-hander materialises. Medina's there, poised to pounce on it like a cat on a rat. Except I paddle into the zone, forcing him to sit there and wait to see if I'll go for it, which I do. Time's up. I'm exhausted, but throw in a giant, elation-fuelled air. The final result:

Wright: 11:97
Medina: 11.77

Make no mistake: if I had stayed out the back and left that wave for Medina, he'd have taken it, nailed it and won. I'm certain of it. It's baffling as to how that wave even came to be. There's this semi-mystical notion in surfing that champions can manifest a wave when they need one, summon a doozy through the power of their mastery and profound connection with the ocean. It sounds far-fetched, I realise, except it seems to happen too often to be coincidence.

Sal greets me on the shoreline, clutching an Australian flag. Even before she chose to pursue surfing, she'd dreamed of being an Olympian in one of the various sports in which she excelled. For her to put aside the dejection associated with her own defeat and be here like this, shining like a Sunday morning, touches me. Not far behind her is the rest of the team. My joy is tinged with amazement and disbelief, because I've succeeded despite the wretched form I brought with me to Japan. Amazement because I've done it in conditions more suited to many of my rivals, and disbelief because nothing like this seemed possible not so long ago when I was laid up with and addled by injury. I've come third but this is the victory of a lifetime.

While I'm still on the beach, dripping wet and holding my board, Jason grabs my arm. He has Kita and the kids on a Facetime call.

'Can you believe it? Can you *believe* it?' I blurt to Kita, who's sobbing. This is her triumph as much as mine.

Vali is there, too, tucking into a tub of ice cream, which is his favourite food in the world, maybe his favourite *thing* in the world.

'What do you reckon, bud?' I ask. 'What's better, eating ice cream or an Olympic medal?'

'Ice cream!' he says, taking another spoonful.

The medal ceremony happens outside in the squalls. Many times in the last four years, including on my darkest days, I'd imagined myself with my arms raised and an Olympic medal around my neck. Now it's happening, and it's so much sweeter than I'd envisioned. Because of Covid, my medal is handed to me, and I hang it myself. When the Australian flag is raised, it's as though my mind separates from my body, and I'm no longer just me but part of a collective national consciousness that is rejoicing in the moment.

Afterwards, I'm talking to the media.

'All the TBI [traumatic brain injury] survivors out there, all the people who have had bad brain injuries, I just want to let you know, it's all possible,' I say.

*

SO, THAT'S MY STORY, but it's not the whole story. Not even close. For that, I need to take you back – not just to getting smashed at Pipeline, or to meeting Kita, or to life on the tour, but all the way back to my boyhood in a little seaside town, where my family and circumstances started shaping me into who I am.

I realise that, for a lot of people, I'm defined by what happened to me at Pipeline – the accident and its aftermath. I accept that. But for it all to make sense, you need more than a graphic account of the incident. I promise not to provide a rundown of every wave I've ever caught, or every board I've ever waxed. I'll stick to the important stuff, in and out of the surf. Join me? Please. Because this is one ride I'd rather not take alone.

PART I

DON'T SHOW YOU'RE HURT

I

AS FAR AS I KNEW, the world was an ocean, blue and endless. Every day, there it was out the front of our home. And there it had always been.

My family lived in a two-storey brick house on a street called The Marina in Culburra, near Nowra on the New South Wales South Coast. In the 1980s, with help from his brothers, mates and one or two tradesmen, my father Rob built this place with his own hands. At the time, it was much too big for just him and my mother Fiona, but their plan was to fill it with children. And that's exactly what they did. Born on 16 January 1990, I have an older brother Tim, two younger sisters Kirby and Tyler, and a kid brother Mikey. Nine years separate Tim and Mikey.

My father was a plumber and fanatical surfer, as was his best mate, Col Cheadle. They bought adjacent beachfront blocks in Culburra at a time when most people in the area preferred to live a street or two back from the sand dunes. My father's attitude was: the closer to the waves, the better. Through the 1990s and beyond, he and Col were among a handful of local dads who helped turn this tiny town of some 1500 people into a surfing hotspot that produced a roll call of high performers.

I got my first surfboard when I was five. A hand-me-down from my uncle Mark, it was lurid green and a bit dinged up, but to my mind it was surfing's version of Excalibur. It was the handiwork of a local legend in board-shaping, Laurie Byrne, who introduced my parents to each other.

When it came to surfing, I was a natural. Within a month of starting, I'd left behind what most little kids do for years – scoot along in the froth, belly-down on their boards. By example, my father and Tim showed me how real surfing was done. I was still only five when I first stood goofy-footed (right foot forward) on my Byrne board and rode assuredly to the shoreline.

As a boy, Tim was just as proficient as I was – and just as hooked. If you wanted to find the Wright brothers, the place to start looking was the ocean out front. Two and a half years older than me, Tim kept an eye on me in what was effectively our playground, and it wasn't long before it was our other siblings' playground, too.

Surfing filled my head. I needed to do it every day. I'd squeeze in a session before the first bell at Culburra Public School. While in class, I'd daydream about an afternoon session, often while doodling waves – perfect barrels, of course, rising majestically out of a glassy sea. Wave drawing: why couldn't *that* have been a subject?

When you fall in love with surfing, you fall in love with all its accoutrements and accessories as well – the boards and boardshorts; the T-shirts, hoodies and wetsuits; the magazines (*Waves, Tracks, Surfing Life*); and the stickers contained in those bibles of surfing. Stickers mattered, and I couldn't get enough of them: every centimetre of my bedroom window was covered in them. As a kid, my blond hair had to be long. Much like it is now, only thicker.

IN THE WRIGHT FAMILY solar system, my father was the sun around which the rest of us revolved. Tall and square-jawed, he was as lean and strong as a gymnast. If there was a gram of fat on his permanently sun-tanned body, you'd have needed a DEXA scanner to find it. He was ripped from all the surfing he did, as well as the diverse exercise routine and bland diet he swore by. My father is a conscientious person who's allergic to short cuts and soft options. For a while, he had fifteen men working for him in the plumbing business he built from scratch.

With his work and five kids, my father had heavy demands on his time, but every June there was an event penned into his diary that was non-negotiable. This was the annual two-week surf trip to Indonesia he made with a group of mates that included Col, our other next-door neighbour Craig White, and another mate Steve Watson. All three had sons around my age – Luke, Keegan and Ty, respectively – who were grommets like me.

Whenever my father spoke about Indonesia, he'd light up. Although often serious and stern, he exuded excitement when one of these trips was approaching. Tim and I were spellbound by his tales of surfing all day with buddies in this strange land, where they'd bump into legends of the sport such as Gerry Lopez and Terry Fitzgerald. To us, Indonesia seemed like Xanadu.

In early 1997, when I was seven and Tim was nine, we started pestering Dad to take us with him that winter to Indonesia. Initially, he was noncommittal.

'Well,' he said, 'if you're going to be well-mannered, and you listen when your mother or I tell you to do something, I could think about taking you with me.'

That was classic Dad. He had a way of bringing everything back to manners, obedience and parental respect. In this case, it was an effective strategy: Tim and I fell right into line for a couple of weeks before renewing our pleas.

'Well,' he said, 'if you can both surf Aussie Pipe, then you can come to Indonesia.'

2

AUSSIE PIPELINE, ALSO KNOWN over the years as Black Rock, is the most revered, readable, consistent but frightening break on the South Coast. Located just south of Jervis Bay on the western point of Summercloud Bay, it's a barrelling, left-handed broken-reef swell that, in truth, only experienced and accomplished surfers should take on. Of course, in our minds, Tim and I fitted that description. As for my father's attitude, he had faith in our abilities. But more than that, he believed in rising above fear, refusing to let it run your life or even influence your choices.

'Lean into fear,' he'd often say to us.

Although my father was typically very strict on us kids, he was much less so whenever surfing was in the frame. When it came to surfing, all the Wright kids were on a long leash. I'm sure this was linked to my father's childhood, when he would cut classes at Jannali Boys' High School in the Sutherland Shire and fare-dodge to surf the southern Sydney beaches with his mates. Apparently, my grandfather used to erupt whenever word of my father's truancy reached him.

'What are you doing, surfing with a bunch of bums?' he'd scold.

But where waves were involved, my father couldn't help himself, and he passed on that affliction to his children.

Like most brothers, Tim and I would often bicker and fight, and occasionally those fights would turn physical. But even when they did, we'd be allies again the instant we heard the approaching footsteps of Mum or Dad.

'All right, don't look hurt,' one of us would tell the other.

We were close. I looked up to Tim and knew I could count on him if I was ever in trouble. And just such a scenario arose during our Aussie Pipe rite of passage.

My father's workday could start as early as 3 am, which meant he usually had some free time in the afternoon. One sunny day in the early autumn of 1997, he collected Tim and me early from school. We made the thirty-minute drive then fifteen-minute walk on a bush trail to reach Aussie Pipe.

As a rule, on the east coast of Australia, the afternoon heralds a nor'-easterly or onshore breeze that reduces waves to unrideable mush. Owing to the peculiar geography of Aussie Pipe, however, a nor'-easter is an offshore wind that combs the swell, holding up the waves so that, by the time they break, they throw themselves outward in resistance, turning them tubular. As a surfer, all you need to do is point your board in the right direction and crouch, and before you know it, you'll be in the green room, man. But you don't want to fall off. Control is everything – you're surfing in shallow water above jagged rock that's covered in barnacles and, more worryingly, sea urchins with spikes that will puncture your skin like needles.

My Aussie Pipe examination was going smoothly until I came unstuck on a five-footer and got flipped over backwards. While getting buffeted underwater, my head struck the reef. Surfacing, the world was a blur. I'd done a number on my right ear, which was bleeding all over the place. Tim spotted me, swum to my side and helped me back to shore, reassuring me as we went. Then he sat with me on the rocks. My father missed the wipeout, but as soon as he noticed his boys out of the water with me looking upset, he left the surf and came over to us.

Looking back on this now, what happened next was significant in the scheme of my life. It helped to foster in seven-year-old me some of the qualities that a professional surfer must possess – bravery, resilience, toughness – but also started the process of turning me into someone who was cavalier, even foolhardy, when it came to managing injury. In no small way, it set me up for catastrophe.

Anyway, I was sitting on this rock, elbows on my knees, head in my hands, busted up with a mangled ear, and my father sat down next to me. He asked me what happened and how I was feeling, then he got down to it.

'You've had a bad wipeout,' he said. 'You're scared of this place now, right? But now's the time to conquer your fear. Right now. This is your chance to show mother nature that you're here, that you're not going to take a backward step, that you're not scared of this wave. You can stand up now or you can let this beat you. That's your choice.'

Except it didn't really feel like a choice.

After a short rest, I re-entered the jaws of Aussie Pipe. I was shit-scared and feeling woozy, but I paddled back out with Tim and my father, and I caught waves until my father could see the apprehension had left my eyes.

When we arrived home, my mother recoiled at the sight of my ear. She cleaned it, dressed it and fussed over me in a way

Dad never would. I went to bed that night, replaying my first serious surfing mishap, but also feeling pleased with myself for not letting it stop me, for eschewing weakness for courage.

The next morning, on re-examining my ear, my mother decided to take me to a doctor, who inserted two stitches. There were two wounds, however, the doctor explained, and he wouldn't be able to repair the other one properly because we'd waited too long.

'This lad should have been taken to a doctor or the hospital straight after the accident,' he said.

The doc said I was probably going to have a little gap in my ear for the rest of my life. And he was right. At the time, though, I didn't much care because I'd earned the right to go to Indo. Tim had, too.

3

LEADING UP TO THE June holidays of 2007 and our trip to
the promised land, Tim and I behaved like choirboys. Setting
the table, saying 'please' and 'thank you' twenty times a day,
taking out the rubbish, helping Mum with Mikey . . . nothing
was too much bother.

Where we were headed was the same spot in Indonesia that
my father and his mates went to every year: Uluwatu, a region
on the southwestern tip of the Bukit Peninsula, Bali, discovered as a surfing location during the making of the classic 1971
surf film *Morning of the Earth*. The journey from Culburra
to Uluwatu took a whole day, but once we were there, the
appeal of our new surroundings was instantly apparent even
to a seven-year-old: azure waters, white sand, limestone cliffs –
and minimal development. There'd be nothing to do here
besides surf.

At home, my father lived simply; in Uluwatu, he took
that practice to a new level. Our home for two weeks was a
surf camp comprising a single, crudely built and dilapidated
wooden eyesore. Our room was on the top floor, and I prayed
silently to be spared a gruesome death every time we negotiated the rickety, hole-riddled stairs. There wasn't even an inside
toilet. My father paid six bucks a night for us to stay in that

dump, and I swear he got ripped off. There was plenty of much nicer accommodation nearby, of course, but roughing it was what my father wanted – for himself and for his boys.

And I wasn't complaining really. The point was, we were there. No school, no commitments and a licence to surf from dawn till dusk. Tim and I rose every day at 4 am, when we'd don our boardies, rashies and reef booties (we were surfing a reef break like Aussie Pipe, so you needed to protect your feet), smother ourselves in sunblock and gobble some rolled oats. At first light, we hit the water. We surfed ourselves to a standstill, coming ashore now and then only to refuel on cheap food. Tim and I spent the whole time amped. I know it sounds corny, but we were the happiest kids in the world to be in Bali.

While we were there, I saw a different side to my father – a happier side, I guess. For him, a life condensed to surfing was a lot easier than the grind of running a business and feeding seven mouths. Not once during that fortnight did he reprimand Tim or me for anything. When it was time to go home, we'd reached an understanding: provided we behaved ourselves, Tim and I could come back to Indonesia every year until the magic wore off. And it never did. Only once I'd qualified for the Big Dance – the Association of Surfing Professionals (ASP) World Tour, in 2010 – did I stop accompanying my father to Uluwatu.

WHEN I WAS EIGHT, my father took me to a Junior Pro competition. I was ecstatic watching these teenagers carve it up, so much so that the guy from Rip Curl who was the running the event, Andy Higgins, noticed me.

'Would you like to do the flag bearing?' he said.

Flag bearing involves changing the flag during heats to alert the competitors they have five minutes left. It's a nothing job for most people, but as a frothing grommet, I was thrilled to take it on and performed it with all the enthusiasm and gravitas of a Wimbledon ball kid.

At the presentation ceremony, the master of ceremonies (MC) called me up to the platform so the crowd could thank me for my efforts.

'What do you want to be when you grow up?' the MC said.

'I want to be a pro surfer.'

That got a big laugh from the crowd, and the MC was chuckling away too. 'What about a flag bearer?' he asked.

I dead-panned the guy. Not a hint of a smile. 'No,' I said. 'I'll be a professional surfer.'

My dad loved that. For him, it was a sign that he was raising a serious-minded kid, who could cut through frivolity and inanity to speak plainly about his intentions. And you know, all I said was that I wanted to be a professional surfer; I didn't say I was aiming to be a world champion one day – even though I was. I had visions of emulating one of my surfing heroes, Tom Carroll, who in 1983 had become the first goofy footer to win a world title.

In the years that followed, as I left behind the naivety of early childhood, I began to understand my father better. It became clear to me – sometimes painfully, other times with a surge of pride – that he was far from your average man.

My father had zero tolerance for swearing or idleness. Unless we were doing schoolwork or helping around the house, he wanted us kids outside – playing sport, exercising, or surfing. To reinforce his expectations, he banned us from watching television. There was a TV in the house, but it was almost never switched on. It's possible he and Mum watched it occasionally when we kids were asleep, but I doubt it because I knew enough even then to know my father is not a hypocrite. We had hardly any toys either. At birthdays and Christmas, he prohibited our aunts and uncles from buying us anything besides books.

My father was a master of martial arts and ran a training school out of our front yard. There were two classes during the week for children, while adults attended on Saturdays. A photo taken at one of those Saturday classes shows my father addressing about fifty students. He would do more than teach the finer points of kung fu, though; he'd lecture on the need for self-discipline and the rewards to be had from abandoning the things you craved but did you no good, like gambling and junk food.

'This feels like a cult,' I heard people say.

Class or not, Dad insisted his kids be up at 4.30 every morning to practise Wu Chi Kung Fu, a blend of martial arts fighting styles. More often than not, we got a repeat dose in the afternoon. How purposefully we approached our kung fu was one of Dad's measuring sticks for how we were performing in life. He wanted to see grit, a thirst for hard work and an outsized pain tolerance.

In our house, if you slept in (which meant later than 4.30 am), Dad would let everyone know about it.

'Owen's slacking off,' he'd announce.

After a while, he didn't need to say things like that much anymore because we'd do the rebuking for him.

'Kirby's slacking off.'

'Tim's got no heart.'

'Tyler's a sack of spuds.'

Daily life became competitive, with public shaming the punishment for anyone who dared steal some post-dawn winks.

Dad was the archetypal taskmaster at these family kung fu sessions, which happened outside in all weather. One torture test involved sinking into a low, wide squat while holding your arms above your head for up to twenty minutes. After a while, your thighs trembled and burned, and your shoulders felt ripe to explode. You'd be dripping sweat and sometimes pleading for mercy, but my father insisted we hold the pose until he gave the order to rise. If you dropped your arms prematurely, you risked copping a whack on the hand or your backside.

Being a girl didn't exempt you from this morning ritual. This was especially tough for Kirby because she was in no way a morning person – man, she zombied her way through most of those workouts. And nor did being a kindergartner: once you were old enough for school, my father believed, you were old enough to learn discipline.

I can laugh about those sessions now, even acknowledge they did me some good. But at the time, they invoked dread, anguish and fear.

Being out and about with my father could lead to embarrassment, like when he'd order us to perform push-ups at the supermarket if we'd annoyed him by whinging or mucking up.

While you hated being down there on the filthy floor making a spectacle of yourself, it never occurred to you to disobey: when Dad gave an order, you followed it.

My father did not consume sugar, coffee, tea, alcohol or meat. Consequently, by paternal decree, the entire Wright family was vegetarian – I suspect we were the only vegetarian family on the South Coast at the time. My mother, who did all the cooking in our house, did her best to serve us appetising meals sans meat, but that was no easy feat night after night. There were times when my siblings and I found dinner close to inedible. Of course, my father had no tolerance for fussiness.

'You can eat what's been cooked for you,' he'd say, 'or you can go hungry tonight and have it for breakfast.'

Although he allowed us to attend birthday parties, we were forbidden to consume what he called 'rubbish' food. Pies, cakes, lollies, biscuits, ice cream, soft drink . . . all were off limits, so we tended to go hungry at parties.

My father had a handful of very close mates, but he didn't make many new ones in the Culburra community on the strength of his child-rearing practices. Laurie Byrne once spoke to him about this, advising Dad to give us more breathing room, and back off on holding us to military standards of self-discipline and restraint. But Laurie might as well have said his piece to a sea wall.

Many people thought our vegetarian diet was madness, telling Dad as much. 'How could your children possibly be getting enough protein?' they'd say.

These questions never fazed my father. 'Watch my kid outrun your kid,' he'd shoot back.

And what could anyone say to that? Because nothing about the way we sprinted, swam, paddled or surfed suggested a hint of malnourishment. Based on real-world evidence, it was hard to make the case that we were burning the wrong kind of fuel.

Some years later, when I was seventeen, I read and reread a book called *Eat Right 4 Your Blood Type* by Dr Peter J. D'Adamo. From my perspective, its key message was that people with type O blood (for example, the Wright family of Culburra) should favour high-protein foods, and eat lots of meat and fish while limiting grains, beans and legumes. Only type A people should avoid meat, D'Adamo argued.

Over a period of months, armed with this evidence, I tried to convince my father that if we, as a family, were to start eating a few serves of meat each week, it could help everyone's surfing, including his own. I didn't think I was getting through, then one afternoon, he arrived home from work carrying a plastic bag from which, unceremoniously, he withdrew a whole chicken.

My response was to grab the bird, hold it to my chest and perform a waltz-like dance around the dining table. Mum roasted it that night as the centrepiece of the heartiest meal that we – I'll speak for all the kids here – ever had the pleasure of eating. Dad tucked in, too, though not quite with the same enthusiasm. That meal was a turning point for me; meat has been a feature of my diet ever since. Dad, on the other hand, soon reverted to vegetarianism.

My father was a hard man when we were kids. Neither showing his emotions nor acknowledging ours was a strong suit. But still, in those early years, I received everything

I needed. I can't speak for my siblings on that point. I suspect that Kirby, Tyler and Mikey would have appreciated a little more paternal empathy, softness and affection. But if there were gaps in his parenting repertoire – and there were – my mother did a fine job of filling them.

4

MY MOTHER AND FATHER are very different people, to the extent that you could wonder how they got together in the first place. Mum was a South Coast native from Currarong, which is about twenty minutes south of Culburra. Though not a surfer, she was a beach girl who'd been in and out of the ocean since she could walk. When she and Dad first crossed paths in their early twenties, he was a fledgling plumber who got around in an old, barely roadworthy truck, while she worked as a nurse at the local veterinary clinic. Dad took an instant shine to this pretty, tender-hearted blonde, and on the advice of his mate Laurie, he kept taking his dog to the vet on spurious grounds.

My mother agreed to go out with him, only to discover that his idea of a first date was a morning's pig-hunting in local scrub. She hated every minute of it and wondered afterwards whether it was worth bothering with this guy. As she saw more of him without a rifle in his hands, however, the attraction became mutual.

Sometimes, one of us kids, feeling daring, would tease our father about how he managed to woo Mum.

'If you know where you're going,' he'd say, 'women are attracted to that.'

35

While Dad's formal education ended after completing Year 10 (or Fourth Form as it was known then), he was no drifter. He became a plumber and started building his sole-trader operation into a thriving enterprise. As soon as he could, he began assembling a workforce and taking on commercial jobs. With his street smarts and Edisonian work ethic, nothing was going to stop him.

I think my mother responded to his ambition because she was also ambitious in her own way. She wanted life to be comfortable and secure for herself and her children, and was often coming up with astute ideas for investments.

Because my father's business absorbed most of his time, the task of ferrying the kids to our various sports fell largely on Mum. Depending on the time of year, we had dawn swimming sessions and afterschool practices for water polo, cricket, football and sundry other active pursuits, culminating in the weekend matches, which might have followed Nippers and surf-lifesaving comps. But the bane of Mum's life was my constant pleading at the crack of dawn for her to drive me (and often a sibling or two) to the beach.

Even though we had the beach right out front, and even though the surf there was often pretty good, the fact is, at any given time, the best surf tended to be to the north at Crookhaven Heads, or to the south at Tilbury Cove. Sometimes, I'd get to those spots by running for twenty minutes – this skinny primary school kid, board tucked under his arm. Other times, I'd make the journey on my bike, wobbling madly because I had only one hand free to steer. But for convenience, nothing compared to being dropped off by Mum; she just needed a little convincing every morning.

'Aaargh, go away,' she'd murmur when I darkened her door at 5 am. My father would be long gone to work by then.

'I'll fix you a cup of tea, Mum,' I'd say, then scurry off to the kitchen.

A few minutes later, I'd reappear with her cuppa and serve it with an ingratiating smile. Then I'd retreat, because my best course of action was to leave her alone to drink it, but I might flick on a light as I went.

Most times, ten minutes later, she'd emerge in the hallway, car keys jingling. She'd drop off Tim and me at 5.30 am and return to collect us about 7.30, so we had just enough time to get ready for school. We'd always be in this almighty rush to make it to the bus stop in time, so Tim and I would take short cuts through neighbours' yards.

On the mornings when Tim and I had to settle for surfing out the front, at about 7.45 am Mum would appear on the balcony and whistle for us to come in. She had a surprisingly powerful whistle, my mum, but Tim and I still felt we could act oblivious and plausibly claim not to have heard her over the breaking waves. Mum would then walk down to the dunes and peel off another ear-piercer, accompanied by some withering eye contact. At this point, Tim and I faced a choice: we could come ashore, or we could turn our backs in defiance.

'We just can't go in,' I'd say to Tim. 'It's too good.'

'Yep. Hold strong. Hold strong. Try not to look at her.'

Later, back at the house, Mum was usually quite relaxed. She wasn't the sort of person who'd sulk over being ignored by her surf-mad boys. Later, Tyler and Mikey would often be part of this caper, too.

Those times when Mum was a bit miffed, we'd just say that she could drop us at school when she headed into town, because she went into Nowra most mornings for groceries or to help Dad with the books. If she wasn't going into town, well, that was our lucky day. Tim and I would high-five each other and scamper back out. There'd usually be Dad to answer to later, but because the trouble revolved around surfing, we could usually handle him, too. Like I told you, surfing was Dad's kryptonite.

MUM WAS ON THE sand when I pulled off my first aerial at age nine. I'd been trying to do one for months – and dreaming of doing one for years – and felt sure it was going to happen this one afternoon. Mum was there poised to capture the moment on film.

Anyway, sure enough, I pumped this two-foot wave for speed, then picked my moment to drive up the face to a breaking lip. When I felt my board leave the lip, I raised my knees so my feet were level with my chest. Airborne, I stayed low and stuck the landing. Sounds easy, right? It's not. Man, I was ecstatic. It felt like my greatest achievement. I raised both arms and claimed it before running up the beach.

'Mum! Did you film it?'

She had – and played it back to me on the spot. The truth was my board had separated from the water by a distance roughly the length of my thumb, but it didn't matter. I was still out of the water. It was still an air.

'Look at you,' Mum said, eyeing the footage. Then she looked at me and gave me the widest, proudest smile – the kind of smile you see in storybooks.

Mum may have had reservations about Dad's parenting style, but she never betrayed them to us. I'm sure there were times when she felt sorry for us, but we were a very traditional family in the sense that my father brought home the bacon and Mum cooked it, so to speak, and they worked well as a team.

5

I WOULDN'T SAY I believe in destiny or predetermination, but I do think the momentum of your life can move so decisively in one direction that there can be only place you're going to finish up.

As well as growing up a stone's throw from the ocean in a family of surfers, I lived next door to an older boy, Luke Cheadle, a fellow goofy footer who was competing at the Australian titles when he was still in school, thus blazing a trail for someone like me. Luke's dad Col, my dad's mate, owned the local surf shop. Even though Luke was several years older than me, we often surfed together. He was a massive charger, fearless, happy to take on un-surfable waves, and I kind of idolised him.

Another piece in the puzzle was sponsorship. Kids who landed a sponsorship . . . oh man, their confidence would skyrocket. The conventional wisdom was that if you wanted to make it one day as a pro, you needed to be sponsored by one of the big three surf companies – Rip Curl, Quik-silver or Billabong – who could get you wildcards into big events down the track. What's more, you needed to get that sponsorship before you turned eleven, or it would probably never happen for you.

As the clock ticked down, getting sponsored became everything to me. As usual, my father stepped up. He reasoned that because Billabong was already sponsoring a Culburra boy, Luke, we'd be best served targeting Rip Curl, with whom I had that tenuous connection courtesy of my flag-bearing work. Dad spliced together a film montage of me surfing at Aussie Pipe and sent it to Rip Curl.

The reply effectively said: *No thanks – get some results and we'll take another look. We don't sponsor every kid who can surf a bit.*

Fine, thought Dad, who always took knockbacks as a challenge.

'Owen, we're going to target the Rusty Gromfest,' he said. 'Win that and you'll get a sponsorship for sure.'

The Rusty Gromfest, held at Lennox Head Beach just south of Byron Bay since the mid-1990s, is the big event for up-and-coming Australian surfers. I showed up in 2000 as a ten-year-old to compete in the boys' 12-and-under division. I took it out and, sure enough, the Rip Curl contract followed hard upon its heels. The initial payola was stickers, a wetsuit, some T-shirts and shorts. I thought I'd gone to heaven. I'd have been happy with just the stickers. I'm still sponsored by Rip Curl to this day.

Would I have ever landed a sponsorship or made my mark in surfing without my father's initiative? I don't know. Many years later, this question came up in a conversation between Tim and me.

'You know,' he said, 'I didn't get the same attention or encouragement from Dad that you did when it came to surfing. As a kid, I remember trying to find a sponsor on my own, whereas Dad did everything for you.'

I didn't know what to say. Tim didn't seem angry or bitter about it; he was very matter of fact. And he made a fair point, too.

6

YOU TAKE LIFE AT face value as a kid. You seldom question why things are the way they are, or whether they could be different or better. Such was my approach to my father's ways.

Looking back, and thinking about what was behind all his rules and rituals, I'm convinced he was trying to create champions. Surfing champions? Well, yes, though not necessarily. That's the road most of us chose to follow – some of us for longer than others, some of us with greater fervour and single-mindedness. But I believe my father's overarching goal was broader than surfing.

What he set out to do, I think, was to develop in each of us a champion's mentality, which we could draw on in whatever field we pursued. Yes, it would be indispensable at the pointy end of competitive surfing. But it would be just as valuable in another sport, in law – or in plumbing for that matter. The champion's mentality, my dad reckoned, was an indispensable means to any worthwhile end.

My father was determined to raise exceptional children who'd grow into exceptional adults. For him, that meant taking an unconventional, though in many ways old-fashioned, approach to child-rearing. He resolved to make us strong of mind, body and spirit. In matters of honesty and loyalty, punctuality and dependability, the lines separating right and wrong were drawn in indelible ink. He told us there was an unbreakable connection between how we conducted ourselves and our capacity to give expression to whatever gifts we possessed.

'The higher your talent grows, the higher your manners grow,' he'd say. 'And the more your manners grow, the higher your talent can go.'

Behind my father's methods was a bedrock of religious belief, but it wasn't a straightforward matter of his being a god-fearing man who followed the dictates of the Bible or Koran. If my father had a sacred text, it was *The Faith I Live By*, by Ellen G. White, a co-founder of the Seventh-day Adventist Church in the United States of America. Knowing that, you may be inclined to pigeonhole him as a Seventh-day Adventist, but that wouldn't be accurate either. My father never went to church and discouraged his children from going. Church, he said, was a refuge for drunks and scoundrels. He also forbade us from attending school scripture classes, which he (quite reasonably) didn't trust to reflect his idiosyncratic take on religious observance.

'If anyone tries to send you to anything like that,' he told us, 'you have my permission to come home. In fact, your mother or I will pick you up. If you find yourself stuck in a scripture class, don't pay any attention.'

When it came to following a righteous path, my father had laid his own, though *The Faith I Live By* was a manual of sorts for him. A daily devotional book first published in 1958, it's a collection of biblical extracts accompanied by commentary from White that clarifies each day's lesson.

As a teen, I did some research into White. She was born in 1827 in Gorham, Maine, and reported having her first divine vision at the age of seventeen. Four years later, she claimed to receive her first 'health-reform vision', which told her to abstain from alcohol, tea and coffee. Later, she added meat and butter to the banned list. Throughout her long life, she often craved meat and could feel feeble for not having it. 'I will not taste a morsel,' she declared in 1870. 'I will eat simple food, or I will not eat at all.'

Simple food for White meant a diet of vegetables, fruit and porridge, which became my father's 'vision' for himself and the rest of us.

So, he didn't go to church or talk to us about Jesus, the resurrection or eternal life, but he kept *The Faith I Live By* on his bedside table and read from it every day. He also prayed a lot – mainly to give thanks and ask for strength – and believed in living simply, honourably and fearlessly.

When I was nineteen, he gave me one of his copies of *The Faith I Live By*. I found it heavy going – the written version of a lot of what I'd been hearing from Dad all my life.

Much has happened to my father since we all lived together in Culburra, but he still has his head in that book every day, sometimes for hours at a time. A while back, he told me that he wished he'd done more to introduce us to God when we were kids, but he'd felt it would be better if we came to faith by our own volition. At this point in our lives, though, none of us seems wired that way.

*

THE APPROACH TO SCHOOL in our house was similarly unusual. You might think my father would have ridden all our humps to realise our academic potential, but that didn't happen. Yes, he wanted us to do well scholastically, but good grades weren't one of his benchmarks for how we were progressing – nor was regular attendance. During primary school, I was often late to class because I couldn't drag myself out of a pumping surf. Likewise, my father allowed me to miss entire days of school to compete in surf competitions. And in high school, I enjoyed even more freedom – sometimes my teachers wouldn't lay eyes on me for weeks at a time.

Dad spelled out his position on this when I was in Year 8.

'I don't mind you missing school, so long as you're doing something worthwhile,' he said, one night at dinner.

'Well, I'm going to surf for six hours a day and train my arse off for another two,' I'd reply. 'You know, get ready for the next comp.'

'Fine.'

After Culburra Public School, I was a pupil at Nowra Anglican College and later at St John the Evangelist Catholic High School, Nowra. I also spent quite some time in a home-schooling arrangement with a great local family, the Hills. They had something like eleven children, most or all of whom were very bright as well as keen surfers. The mother Sue ran the show, but several of her kids chipped in as tutors, as did Tim.

Of all the Wright kids, Tim was the only one you would describe as a dedicated student. Semi-dedicated might be more accurate because, for Tim like the rest of us, nothing held a candle to surfing. Unlike me, however, my older brother could look at, say, a capital 'C' and not see the outline of a wave.

Dad took note of this; eventually, he started grooming Tim to take over the family plumbing business. Tim had done his plumbing apprenticeship under Dad, but he wasn't keen on heading up the family business anytime soon. His attitude was that he'd rather start at the bottom somewhere else, away from Dad's sometimes overbearing presence. He was a plumber for a while before dabbling in a bunch of fields, including sports management and film editing. In his mid-twenties, he started a law degree and has been working as a solicitor for a few years now.

Back in 2005, you were allowed to leave school at fifteen. That's what I did, with my father's blessing. Just as he was okay with my skipping school, so long as I was busy, he was also happy for me to leave it altogether without a certificate, provided I had a plan. And I did. I was going to be a pro surfer.

7

IN THE TEN YEARS after I first carried a board into the ocean, surfing evolved to mean different things to me. Initially, it was playtime, a source of joy untainted by my own or others' expectations. I fell in love with surfing movies. I watched them on repeat with my mates and sometimes my father, who could be persuaded to relax his TV ban occasionally if it meant another screening of one of the G-Land films from the 1990s. He was okay with me watching surf movies that were pure surfing, but those that had a pervasive anti-Establishment vibe or scenes of partying, drinking and what he called 'punkish' behaviour weren't allowed in the house.

Surfing kids quickly pick up terms like 'air' and 'barrel' and get wrapped up in them. You hear older guys raving about their 'barrel in Bali' or some such, and to young ears it sounds magical. Consequently, 'getting barrelled' becomes your highest aspiration. Imagine it! To freefall off the crest of a wave; skate through its hollow section as it breaks; disappear for two, five, seven seconds behind a curtain of water; and re-emerge still planted on your board. What could be more exhilarating?

When you're a little kid, surfing inside a barrel is beyond you. So you aim for shorey barrels, where instead of trying to enter a tube on your feet, you go in on your stomach without even a board, just body-bashing. Later, when you get what seems like your first genuine, fully fledged barrel, you feel invincible; you feel like you're one of the professionals now, even if the reality is you just scraped the edge of the tube – what we sometimes refer to disparagingly as a 'head dip'.

This beginner phase is the purest phase. Alas, it can't last. In my case, before long, it wasn't enough for surfing to be fun; I had to be good at it. Who am I kidding? Not just *good* – crazy-good.

I entered my first comp when I was ten, in Wollongong. Another entrant was Matt Wilkinson (Wilko) – from Copacabana on the New South Wales Central Coast – who became a mate and fellow traveller on the junior and elite tours. I was so geed up in the comp that I caught ten waves in fifteen minutes and had to sit out the last five minutes, because ten was the maximum you were allowed to catch. Trust me: no one catches ten waves in ten minutes. I went berserk out there because it felt like my whole life had been a prelude to that heat. It was agony to stand on the beach and watch the other guys compete with the chance of beating me; I thought I'd blown it. But I won that competition, and I was truly, irreversibly hooked.

So began my life as a competitive junior surfer. For the next seven years, my best and worst times were on the road as my father ferried me, often alongside two or more of my siblings, to comps on the eastern seaboard. We started out in the family's Toyota Tarago, which Dad later swapped for an old ambulance that gave us more space for boards and supplies. Finally, he forked out for a mini school bus that the previous owner had decked out with beds in the back. We travelled around in those various people-movers like the Partridge family. Like I said, I missed a lot of school because of those trips – as did Tim, Tyler and Mikey. Most of the comps were held over four or five days, but none of us ever complained.

While most other grommets and their parents would check into local lodgings, we Wrights lived out of our vehicle. This had nothing to do with a shortage of money. Everyone knew Rob Wright had a pile of cash stashed somewhere – he'd pulled down good money for years – but he never spent a cracker on what he deemed luxuries, which included a proper bed and a square meal from an eatery. Dad would steer us into the carpark of the nearest surf or footy club, and we'd use the facilities there for showering, brushing our teeth and, in Dad's case, shaving.

Being on the road didn't stop my father from practising his tai chi in a park every morning. Often, I'd be there next to him doing the same moves while hoping none of my competitors was watching. At other times, I'd tell myself that these rituals were giving me a competitive advantage – and who cared what anyone thought?

By this stage, we kids were resigned to vegetarian eating, but while that could be tolerable at home with Mum doing the cooking, it was often murder on the road without her. For breakfast, my father would crack raw eggs into bowls of oats and add water or maybe a little soy milk if we were lucky. That was it. *Dig in, kids.* For lunch and dinner, he used a little portable gas-burner to boil vegetables. These were usually served undercooked or soggy because Dad was a candidate for world's worst cook. Occasionally, though, his efforts hit the spot and we'd hungrily tuck into plates of boiled potato and kumara, corn, carrots, beans and maybe some brown rice. All that was missing was meat and any hint of sauce or seasoning, because to my father's mind, flavour was a luxury.

8

THE CLEAN EATING AND sleeping rough, the lectures and dawn martial arts sessions were all part of my father's grand plan to nurture champions. To this end, he had solid raw materials to work with: as surfers, all five kids had talent.

Tim was my equal when we were boys – it's just that I was younger, so it always seemed like I had more potential. Tyler and Mikey were both gifted beyond belief. Kirby was an excellent, Billabong-sponsored surfer – and she could have succeeded on the tour had she persisted – but the intensity of competition and the grind required to keep improving turned her off surfing for a living. Kirby was also a social teenager – probably as much as the rest of us put together.

My father worked like a Trojan to build up his business to the point where, in his mid-forties, he could take off contentedly on our road trips and leave its operations in the hands of trusted lieutenants. We didn't go to every competition, however, because Dad believed in gracing only those events that he judged to be worthwhile.

'You don't wield your axe repeatedly,' he said. 'You strike once and cut well.'

As a junior, from eight to eighteen, I rarely lost at any level of competition. Few boys could match me in terms of hours of surfing in the bank, skills or competitive will.

My father's and Laurie's breathless tales of Banzai Pipeline had established it in my mind as surfing's pinnacle. The ultimate wave. The barrel against which all others are judged. 'But don't listen to the fear stories,' my father would say. 'Pipe is your friend.'

In case you don't know, Pipeline is a reef break located off Ehukai Beach Park, Pupukea, in the cradle of surf culture – the North Shore of the Hawaiian island of Oahu. It consists of three separate reefs, each of which produces consistently violent tubular waves in the autumn and winter.

I was thirteen when I first set eyes on Pipeline. Rip Curl liked to take its hottest prospects to Pipe so they could imbibe its mystique. Rip Curl also wanted to check that its best kids had the necessary mettle to advance to the elite ranks one day – that they wouldn't crumble in the face of Pipeline's power. That's not to say that, as a promising grommet, you'd be tossed into the surf irrespective of the conditions; you wouldn't be allowed to get wet on the rougher days. But even in its quieter moods, Pipe has a way of peeling back any façade of bravado and revealing what lies beneath. Would it be courage, a dare-devil's spirit? Or something else, portending a career dead-end?

On that first trip to Pipe, the surf was huge and I could only watch as more experienced surfers took on its fury. I watched not with fear but with envy.

Two years later, back at Pipe at the age of fifteen, I was able to show people what I was made of. I was standing outside the Rip Curl House, the place where Rip Curl-sponsored athletes stay during Pipe, as the pro surfers debated whether it would be wise to head out that day in ten-foot surf. Me? To much astonishment and some amusement, I grabbed my board and charged. There wasn't a doubt in my mind – I was going to surf. The following year, I was given a wildcard to compete at Pipeline and made it through my first heat. That was four years before I qualified for the tour.

WHEN I WAS FOURTEEN, I won my fourth Rusty Gromfest title, which is when Rip Curl invited me to appear in an arty short film they were shooting starring Mick Fanning, called *Mick, Myself & Eugene*.

About a third of the way into the movie, I make my appearance, grinning from ear to ear in the passenger seat of a 4WD as Mick drives us to a break in Kalbarri, Western Australia. In the voiceover, Mick says, 'Surfing with grommets is funny, especially grommets that get really stoked on surfing. I did a trip with little Owen, and he'd just always be going, "Can we surf? Can we surf?" And I'd be like, "Just settle down, grommet."'

Next, there's some footage of me surfing – pretty well for a kid if you don't mind me saying – then I'm out of the water peeling off my wetsuit, still smiling like a kid at Christmas.

'What do you reckon the waves'll be like tomorrow?' Mick says.

'Smokin',' I say. 'I reckon there'll be pits, just pits all around.' This basically means lots of barrels to hook into.

'Are you excited?'

'Yep,' I say. 'Don't think I'll sleep tonight.'

Behind the scenes, Mick was unfailingly nice to me, though at the same time, I caught glimpses of his dedication. We were in a café for breakfast one morning when a waitress came to take our order.

'I'll have the eggs, the plate of fruit and the muesli,' he said.

'Why you gettin' all that?' I asked him.

'What's that?'

'Why you gettin' everything on the menu?'

'I'm trying to eat a balanced diet.'

'Oh, right.'

Over the course of a few days, I asked Mick roughly 1 million questions about surfing, and he gave me roughly 1 million illuminating answers. Whatever he knew, whatever he'd learned, he was happy to share. Later, I came to realise there were two Micks: the helpful, caring, almost fatherly Civilian Mick, and the fire-breathing Competitor Mick. Man, when that guy was preparing to paddle out for a heat, he looked like he wanted to eat you alive. Headphones on, game face activated, exuding a fuck-off vibe, he was intensity personified. And I liked that. I respected that. I'm cut from the same cloth.

I came across as a carefree kid in that film, but really, I wasn't. Like I said, your relationship with your sport evolves, and I came to set such high standards for myself that I could easily unravel in private, even during comps at which the neutral observer would have said I was in a class of my own.

I'd have meltdowns after winning heats because I was dissatisfied or disgusted with the way I'd surfed. I'd cry in the bus on the night before finals, sick to my stomach with worry that I would show up the next day, make stupid mistakes and lose. Thinking back on those times, it was perfectionism run riot.

I'd go out the next day and win, but still I wouldn't be satisfied.

Though I could be a headcase in my teens, I could always talk to my father.

'This isn't how I want to be surfing. I'm out of rhythm. I'm not getting 8s. I'm not getting 9s.'

'Well, have you been listening to your mum? Have you been waking up early and making your bed? Have you been tidying your room?'

'Yeah, yeah.'

'Those things keep the discipline in your life, son. They're things you can control. Other things you can't.'

'I'm doing those things. I'm winning but . . .'

'The better you conduct yourself, the better results you'll get. But the moment you get those results, you need to be better again in your life, otherwise you'll stagnate. Be better, surf better. Surf better, be better.'

At the time, his advice could be confusing, but I look back on it now as wise. Self-improvement is a ladder with no top rung, he was saying.

Dad would never heap praise on me when I won. If I were lucky, I might get, 'Yep, good job,' and if he was proud of me, it didn't show. His attitude was less: *You're only as good as your last surf*, and more: *You're only as good as your next surf.*

He didn't waste words, my father. Life was about doing, not talking about, the next challenge, having let go of the one just met. The solitary reward for victory might be single-scoop ice cream cones for me and whoever of my brothers and sisters were there, which Dad bought at a milk bar. Given my father's beliefs around diet, this was a colossal concession on his part, and an equally colossal treat for us.

Did I yearn for his approval? That yearning came later as a young adult on the tour, at those times when I was on a hot streak but getting little or nothing from him by way of commendation. I'd think, *Why isn't he happy? Isn't this enough?* But as a youngster, being able to count on him to pick me up when I was low tended to cancel out his shortcomings as a cheerleader. He could always calm me down and lift my spirits by hearing me out and offering solutions, which amounted to ticking off the same old tasks and courtesies.

One time, after a late-afternoon surf out the front at Culburra – I might have been just fifteen at the time and in a bit of strife at school – my father and I sat down in the sand and gazed out to sea as dusk descended and the clouds turned pink.

'You're surfing like an angry teenager these days,' he said. 'You're taking wipeout after wipeout as though that's what you want.'

'I don't know,' I said. 'Maybe. I don't realise I'm angry until I'm out there.'

'That's what the ocean does. It holds up a mirror to your subconscious. If you teach yourself to look and listen, if you can build a relationship with the ocean, it will tell you how you are within yourself.'

From treating the sea as a playground to then as an arena, I later came to see it as something else again: a haven. Many times, I paddled out past the breakers not with the intention of catching waves, but simply to sit on my board in peace and

60

solitude and to think, *How am I travelling? What am I feeling? What do I want?* On the face of it, the last question seemed the easiest to answer: to be a surfer, maybe the best in the world. But was pursuing that goal going to make me happy? That was a different question entirely. And I didn't know the answer.

My surfing only improved after I left school and shone on the Australasian Pro Junior circuit. The buzz among the shrewder judges was that I was probably the best young male surfer in the country and possessed the tools to make it professionally before long. In 2006, aged sixteen, I made that appearance as a wildcard at Pipeline. In May 2007, I reached the quarter-finals at the Quiksilver International Surfing Association (ISA) World Junior Surfing Championships in Costa de Caparica, Portugal. In June 2008, at the same event, this time held on France's southwest coast, when I was eighteen and Tyler just fourteen, we spearheaded a victorious Australian team.

The world, it seemed, was at my feet.

9

'I'VE GOT SOMETHING TO tell everyone,' my father said at dinner one night.

It was the spring of 2008, not long after Tyler and I had returned from France. I'd been feeling quite pleased with myself.

'We'll be leaving Culburra,' Dad announced. 'Your mum and I have bought a house in Lennox Head, across the road from Boulder Beach, and we'll be moving up there.'

Again, vintage Dad. No discussion. No, *how would you feel if we were to . . . ?* Just, *here's what's happening.* A fait accompli.

I faded out as Dad sketched a few details in response to questions from the others. I couldn't see one good reason for uprooting. I was happy here, in the only place I'd known with the surf out front and my mates close by. I'd recently got my driver's licence, too, so now I had mobility and independence in a town I knew like my own face.

At the table that night, I made no attempt to conceal my feelings. I didn't say much, but I was scowling. I'm not sure Dad even noticed, but Mum did. She's since told me she's never seen me so angry. I sulked for days, telling anyone who'd listen that I was going to stay put, though how that would have worked I didn't know.

My father has never been one to justify himself. In his mind, he'd made a decision that was in the best interests of the family of which he was the head, and that was that. But I demanded to know his reasons. *Why do we have to move? And why now?*

To be nearer to the action, my father said. Lennox Head was part of the Northern Rivers of New South Wales – a region that along with the neighbouring Gold Coast was the hot zone of Australian surfing, drawing in the best pros like ants to sugar. Mick Fanning, Joel Parkinson, Dean Morrison, Steph Gilmore . . . all would be roundabouts.

'Look, you know Lennox Head from Gromfest,' Dad said. 'It's a great spot.' Living there would massively cut our travel time to and from most events, he continued. And the surf would be warmer, which Tyler and Kirby liked the sound of but meant nothing to me.

Do kids ever want to move? Kids will always prefer the familiar. It's adults who need change, adults for whom life can begin to feel stale, repetitive or pointless. Okay, at eighteen I wasn't a kid anymore, but I was still living under my parents' roof. I suppose you're a kid until that changes.

There were a few months between Dad's announcement and the scheduled moving date, in which time the real rationale for upping sticks became clearer.

In snippets scattered through various conversations, Dad revealed that he wanted to get me out of Culburra because he believed I was entering a potentially perilous phase of life, a phase in which I could easily self-sabotage my prospects. My mates had developed the usual interest in drinking, partying and generally getting up to mischief. If he could take me up north, Dad reasoned, he could separate me from that destabilising scene and keep me focused on my surfing. Used to being the principal influence in my life, he could see the balance of power shifting towards my peer group and he didn't like it.

Until recently, I'd been living life very much by the book – Dad's book. I was an obedient kid. But I'd started to break out and resist his rigid approach to clean and righteous living. This caused some monumental blow-ups between us. One Sunday morning after, for me, a lively Saturday night, Dad was ropeable.

'Damn it, you know the difference between right and wrong!' he roared.

'Yeah, and I'm not doing anything wrong!' I yelled back. 'I'm just having a bit of fun for the first time in my fucking life.'

'No, no. You know what you're doing, and you know you're on the wrong track.'

One difference between my siblings and me was that I was prepared to take Dad on. By this point, I was no longer scared of him, and I'd stand up to him. I'd challenge him to justify his methods, from the restrictions he placed on what we could eat to his unwillingness to let teenagers act their age.

'You hold me to such high standards,' I said. 'You make out like my life will collapse if I don't do things your way all the time. You reckon my surfing will go to shit. But these other kids are getting the same results that I'm getting without living like monks.'

Another time, I was boiling over while we were standing out the front of the house, and mocked his approach to religion.

'You believe in your stuff. Well, I can go and believe in this tree here,' I said. 'This tree is going to give me all my confidence. This tree is going to tell me whether I'm doing right or wrong.'

A few times, I was so angry that I physically challenged him, and we'd end up on the floor wrestling. While I'd say that neither of us truly wanted to hurt the other, these spirited grapples had Mum and my sisters looking on aghast.

It was a difficult time for Mum, who'd invariably backed my father in disputes, at least in front of us kids. But by then, she could see I'd reached an age when the reins needed loosening. Poor Mum: she was torn. Should she speak up on her son's behalf or continue to take an approach of: *my husband, right or wrong?*

When I'd stayed out till all hours, drunk too much and was too hung over to take part in the morning's martial arts or even to surf, Dad would sometimes express his displeasure: 'You're losing your way!' But more often, he'd retreat into a sullen silence that could last for days and put frost on the windows. Mum could be ticked off with me, too, but mostly I sensed from her a tacit acknowledgement that I was growing up and it was to be expected that I'd seek to push the boundaries.

'You know,' she said one time, 'it would be all right, love, if you had a rest for a bit. It would be okay not to get up at 4 am sometimes.'

If Mum was a sometime ally, then Tim was a brother in arms. He'd had such a gutful of living under Dad's rules that, at the age of nineteen, he'd taken off to live with friends on the other side of the country in Margaret River.

'I can't do this anymore,' he told me, as we headed out for a surf one morning.

Once Tim was gone, it felt like he was out of sight and out of mind for my father, while I, the next oldest and perhaps Dad's Great Hope, was now foremost in his thoughts.

One night, I headed out with a bunch of mates, and we hit the grog like returning sailors. After staggering home in the small hours, I crashed on a mattress in the living room and ended up vomiting in my sleep. I awoke to my parents' undisguised disgust.

That unedifying scene was a turning point because while I was mopping up my puke, I decided I wouldn't be going with my family to Lennox Head. Instead, I would move into a unit on the Gold Coast that I'd bought a year earlier as an investment with my Rip Curl sponsorship money on the advice of my father. Tim had recently left Western Australia and was living there by himself, paying me rent. I figured I'd move in with him. I'd still be leaving Culburra, of course, which would be sad, as would separating from my friends and family, including Dad, but at least I'd be going out on my own while having my big brother alongside me to smooth my transition to parent-less living.

I can't honestly remember what their reaction was to my plan. I was so violently opposed to the move to Lennox Head that I was blind to anyone else's feelings. On the day I left Culburra, I left without fuss. My thoughts were already focused on a new and freer life in which I called the shots.

PART 2

IT'S ALL RIGHT TO GET LOST

10

THE FIRST MONTH OR SO in Coolangatta was like a holiday. Being out and about at night with Tim, rising when I felt like it, eating for taste and taste alone ... these were small but exhilarating pleasures. I still had the surf close by – you could see part of the Snapper Rocks break from the unit – even if it was many times more crowded than Culburra's break, and enough money from my Rip Curl sponsorship and Tim's rent to live comfortably. By this stage, I had my own set of wheels, too. A new Mercedes-Benz Vito van wouldn't have been my first choice – Dad had taken charge of that purchase shortly before I left home – but I had no complaints either.

Is there anything quite so exquisite as newly acquired freedom? I didn't go crazy with mine, but nor I did I spend my nights poring over *The Faith I Live By* or playing Scrabble.

Just as he did when we were kids, my brother looked out for me. Whenever he had plans for the night, which was most nights, he invited me to tag along, usually to one or more of the Gold Coast's myriad bars and clubs. As a result, Tim's friends – he had plenty, and they were all welcoming and easy-going – soon became my friends, if they weren't already. The joys of socialising and connecting with new people were a revelation. Up to that point, I'd spent almost every waking moment focused on surfing. To no small extent, I'd lived the life of a child prodigy. You wouldn't have called me a loner – back in Culburra, I had a few very close mates. But I'd been part of nothing like this network of people with diverse interests.

My diet underwent a similarly seismic shift. All those years of subsisting on vegetables had turned me violently against them. I couldn't abide having anything green or earthy on my plate. Armed with supermarket receipts entitling us to two-for-one deals, Tim and I would hit up the local pub at every chance for a cheap dinner. Whatever the special was, we'd have it, but for me nothing compared with a chicken parmigiana. Honestly, crumbed bird drowned in tomato sauce and melted mozzarella with chips after years of vegetables? You'd be excited too, right?

Yep, life was swell. There was just one problem: my surfing results were going to shit. The slide had started while I was still in Culburra and beginning to spread my wings; now, it was accelerating at a clip. Used to winning on the junior circuit, I was now flopping wherever I went. Each loss was a fresh and piercing blow to my self-image; each loss was a reason to question everything about myself – my true level of talent, my capacity to deal with pressure and adversity, and most gallingly, my ability to succeed without my father telling me what to do and how to live.

I was surfing okay on my own with nothing at stake, but in competition, my level of performance nosedived at times to the point of being embarrassing. To a fellow surfer watching from the sand, I would have looked like someone out of rhythm with the ocean. Some waves I missed, some I should have left alone, others I fell off, others I stayed on but failed to link my turns efficiently or else turned sluggishly. But on the inside, I was out of sorts. I'd departed too quickly and too radically from a way of life that, whether I cared to admit it or not, was bloody good for my surfing.

Amid this slump, I rocked up to the Coffs Harbour Pro Junior. Suddenly, I felt good again. I was sure things were about to turn around because my confidence had returned. Then I got out there and finished dead last. I was struggling to notch a 4. I proceeded to put a few of those dismal results back to back, getting smoked by guys who, frankly, weren't in my league. In people's puzzled looks, I perceived the question: *Holy shit, what's happened to this guy?*

Previously, my father had been on the beach whenever I surfed competitively. But after I went off on my own, he stopped coming so much. Was he keeping track of my results, though? You bet he was. And he was making an example of me to Kirby, Tyler and Mikey.

'You see,' he'd tell them, having detailed my latest flameout, 'Owen's not on the right track, and this is what happens.'

To be fair, he'd say the same thing or similar on the phone to me – or to my face when I visited my family. 'You're all over the place, son.' He is not a sniper, my father. You could never accuse him of talking behind your back.

SO, AFTER LESS THAN three months as a free man, I was in crisis. As nice as parts of my new life were, I had to consider the possibility that living like this could be the ruin of me. It seemed like yesterday I was on the cusp of transitioning from juniors to the big leagues. Now, I looked in danger of becoming just another promising grommet who never amounted to jack. The frustration was enough to have me yelling at myself in the shower. To my mind, I'd been doing only what most people do, indeed what a lot of junior surfers do. I'd watched my fellow competitors gobble chain-store burgers and soft drinks, then show up the next day and surf like Rabbit Bartholomew. But in my case, these same activities seemed to be making me a shell of the surfer I once was.

I had a choice: I could live freely until my money ran out while bidding 'adios' to reaching the tour, or I could revert to my old life of prohibitions and routines – a professional sportsman's life before I was even a professional sportsman. While neither option appealed, I couldn't pretend that surfing results had ceased to matter to me, or that I could envisage a time when they wouldn't. It didn't help that my father was so disapproving of my choices; that his disapproval seeped from his pores; or that he was indifferent, it seemed, to my needs as a teenager as opposed to an athlete.

For a brief time, I thought, perhaps there was a third option – a halfway house between utopia and home detention. What if I stayed here in Coolangatta, but cut out the carousing as competitions approached? Perhaps that would do the trick.

It didn't.

So, one Saturday morning in December 2008, right after breakfast, I packed a few things, climbed into the Vito and headed south towards Lennox Head. I needed to see my father. Forget chicken parmy. Better serve me a whopping piece of humble pie.

11

THOUGH I HADN'T PHONED ahead to say I was coming, my father seemed unsurprised to see me. He filled two glasses with water from the fridge and pointed to the deck. Against a backdrop of our sun-drenched yard and endless bush, we sat opposite each other at the table, both of us tight-lipped as we sipped our waters and listened to the whistling of two rainbow lorikeets that perched on a handrail a few metres away.

'Look, Dad,' I said at last, 'I haven't been getting the results I want. I need to make some changes.'

By now, I was kind of slumped in my chair, mainly looking down. Dad, in contrast, was suddenly very puffy-chested, which didn't make this any easier.

'Yeah, like, I've been getting very average results.'

'Sure,' Dad said. 'That's what comes from an average approach to life: average results.'

It was far from the first time he'd used that line on me, but where in the past I'd pushed back – countered with something like: 'Just because I want to live a little, doesn't make me average' – this time I zipped it. That debate had been won and lost, and we both knew it.

'Yeah, I guess I've been going to parties, drinking too much, not getting out of bed early enough, not eating right, not sticking to disciplined schedules.'

It was funny: the more I spoke, the more I slumped. But the more Dad heard, the more bushy-tailed he became. He'd been waiting for this confessional and was savouring every syllable. He was always going to bathe in a sense of righteous vindication, but did he have to do it in front of me?

'I still reckon my commitment has been higher than everyone else's, but not high by your standards, or mine, I guess. Look, I need you.'

That was a lot for me to admit. But it was only the beginning of our reconciliation. As I bunked at the house, our talks spanned three days.

'What is it you want to achieve, Owen?'

'I want to qualify for the tour,' I said.

This made my father smile. 'And I can help you with that,' he said. 'But it'll be on my terms. You've done things your way this year and you can see where that's got you. Now, we'll do things my way.'

Come the evenings, we'd talk in my room, my father standing and sometimes pacing as he spelled out his plan for my resurgence. I sat on the edge of the bed with a notebook in my lap, dutifully recording his every thought. We pinpointed the events I'd target in 2009 – the Pro Juniors first, then open comps in the Qualifying Series (QS). We tacitly agreed that my father would serve as my coach, and mentor and accompany me to all events. We explicitly agreed that I'd be leaving my Coolangatta apartment forthwith and moving in with my family at Lennox Head.

Clearly, I wouldn't be so much starting a new life as reverting to my old one, just from a different base.

It was around this time that my father gave me a copy of *The Faith I Live By* – the book I was telling you about. For every day of the year, there was a piece of guidance or encouragement. The entry for 9 January, for example, lamented how 'men are absorbed in the pleasures and pursuits of sense'. No one could have accused my father of such a thing.

THE TURNAROUND IN MY fortunes came quickly. In early 2009, I rattled off wins at the first five Pro Junior events. My form caught the eye of the local press, which figured this would be the right time to cover the Wright family's migration to the Northern Rivers. The *Northern Star* ran a puff piece under the headline 'Location just Wright for family of surfers'.

Accompanying the story was a photo taken on our deck, showing my father sitting arrow-straight at the table, nursing his usual glass of water. Opposite him are Mum and Kirby, while sitting on the ground in front of them are Tyler, Mikey and our labradoodle, Oreo. (I'm absent – I was off surfing that day.) Everyone's smiling.

The reporter wasn't there to dig up dirt. 'If you ever wanted a sporting family to move into your region, it would be the Wright family,' his story begins.

Tyler hinted at simmering tensions when she told the reporter that Culburra would always be her home. 'It's great we've moved to Lennox Head,' she said, 'but my roots are in Culburra. That's where I grew up and matured, learned to surf and learned to do surf lifesaving.' Amen to that.

There was no mention in the story of the period I spent on the Gold Coast, or of Tim abandoning the family home when he was nineteen. It was all roses and rainbows.

That said, I have mostly good memories of 2009. My father and I travelled to some twenty events. It was usually just the two of us, though sometimes Tyler or Mikey or both came along.

Morning tai chi and tests of stamina and strength resumed. There was no flying to events, even those in Tasmania, for which the family bus would take a ride on the *Spirit of Tasmania*. On the road, we never went to restaurants or hotels – we'd eat and sleep in our mobile home. I had one bowl, one plate and one set of cutlery, which I'd rinse under a tap at the end of every meal. Laundry involved soaping up the clothes you were wearing and letting the sun dry them off. It could be freezing at night in some parts of the country, in which case you'd keep adding layers of clothing. I wouldn't tolerate it now, but that's because you soften up as you get older. At the time, it was all just life – a life devoid of nights out, alcohol . . . and flavour-some food.

'No sugars, no sauces,' Dad said. 'Simple.'

Simple and bland, I thought. I could have cried or pressed on. I pressed on.

Life runs smoother when you're winning, of course, and in 2009, I won a lot. Dominating the juniors was one thing, but there were grander triumphs to come.

Responding to my hot streak, Rip Curl gave me wildcards into several ASP World Tour events. In April, in Round 2 of the Rip Curl Pro Bells Beach on Victoria's Great Ocean Road, I found myself one-on-one in a Round 2 heat with a thirty-seven-year-old Kelly Slater. At the time, he had won nine of his eleven world titles and was the defending world champion.

Kelly claimed his first pro tour event when I was two years old. He was my father's exemplar of the ultimate surfer. For Dad, what made Kelly untouchable was more than just his surfing ability, though this was – and remains – otherworldly. It was also how Kelly lived, eschewing alcohol, parties and cheap thrills for marathon surf sessions, physical training (including Brazilian jiu-jitsu) and a pristine diet.

When he was a small boy in Florida, Kelly's mother told him, 'Look around you. I'll be surprised if you see anyone successful who's an alcoholic or does drugs. It just doesn't lead anywhere good.' Those words sunk in and, without knowing it, Kelly would grow up to conduct himself like the star graduate of the Rob Wright School of Life.

In terms of surfing's stylistic progressions over the years, Kelly has been either at the vanguard or among the first to achieve mastery. In pursuit of wins, he's left nothing to chance. No one has analysed surf conditions as meticulously as Kelly has, or experimented as imaginatively and fruitfully with board choice and technology. And – how can I put this? – the guy knows how to win. He will *find a way.* He'll sniff out a wave when he most needs it, and pull off a Hail Mary manoeuvre at the death. He's done this time and again. And it's not luck. It's part of Kelly Slater's genius, a product of his magnificent obsession with surfing, and it's driven generations of surfing also-rans to the brink of implosion.

That morning at Bells, I forced down my usual bowl of rolled oats in water. I'd been following my dad's program to the letter. Knowing that, and winning as regularly as I was, I was feeling sure of myself even though my opponent was Kelly. One effect of Dad's program was that it sucked any uncertainty out of my thinking. When I stuck to it, I had a firm conception of who I was and what I wanted.

I reckon only my father and I believed I could win. Everyone else would have figured that this kid (me) would feel privileged just being in the same ocean as the maestro. But that's not how I felt at all. I was excited, but not starstruck. I'd been surfing at least once and often twice a year at Bells since I was eleven. I knew its character and nuances as well as Kelly did.

Shortly before the heat, Dad pulled me aside.

'I know everyone says, "Don't look this guy in the eye," that he's a master of mind games and his gaze will turn you to jelly. Forget that,' Dad said. 'It doesn't apply to you. The reason we train the way we do, the reason we have the discipline we have, is to take on guys like this. Most guys are scared to look at him because they're average. And because they're average, he can look straight through them, see their fear and reverence. When he looks at you, son, he's not going to be able to look through you, because he's going to see a man who expects to win. That's the difference.'

A few minutes later, Kelly and I were sniffing out the first wave. I turned my head to check on him and his blue eyes locked onto mine. No doubt about it: he was measuring me up. I returned his gaze, unblinking and unfazed, until he looked away, not because I'd stared him down (I wasn't delusional) but because he realised, I suspect, that I couldn't be psyched out, that he'd have to beat me with his prodigious skills.

The surf was pumping at about two metres. The conventional wisdom on Bells is that it's a tough break for goofy footers. But I wasn't thinking that way. I was among the first crop of juniors with solid experience there, and I had a plan. This involved doing a bunch of floaters (where you ride over and along the top of a broken part of a wave, then back down onto the open face). And everything worked. I surfed that heat as though I knew Bells like my own bathtub. The waves were fast and fat, and I floated over the top of the lips. I'd land close to the breaking part of the wave then squeeze in extra turns while everyone else raced along the line to get out in front of the wave.

With the clock ticking down, my two-wave score was 14.67. Kelly was in the hunt – and he was surfing well, of course, sliding into barrels at will – until a failed exit on a double-barrel cost him. This no-chance kid had become the GOAT slayer.

Back on the beach, I was stunned: *How the hell did I just do that?* But despite his admiration for Kelly, my father might as well have watched me cook a chop. *No big deal,* his face said. *Just another win. Nothing I didn't expect. Nothing to see here.*

Dad went into control mode; he could see I was elated even though the job wasn't done – this was just a Round 2 heat. Guys wanted to backslap and high-five me, but my father caught my eye and shook his head, subtly but firmly. *Don't! Don't get distracted by this bullshit. This win is just a step towards where we want to go.*

I didn't win at Bells. At that stage, I wasn't ready to go all the way in a tour event. But I kept excelling in the QS.

In June, I won the Sri Lankan Airlines Pro in the Maldives, beating American Pat Gudauskas in a final whose quality seemed to mesmerise onlookers. In two-metre waves, we both surfed as though divinely inspired, me pipping him 19.23 to 18.93. Gudauskas said he was so thrilled with the way he'd performed that he felt like he'd won, even though he'd lost. If you'd reversed the placings, I'd have felt the same way.

Or maybe not. Because that victory meant I'd now accrued enough points in the QS to qualify for the 2010 tour. From arriving broken and humiliated on my father's doorstep just five months earlier, I'd done what I set out to do at age eight.

My reaction? Ecstasy.

The buzz? *Inside Sport* reported this comment from Dane Jordan, the ASP Australasia Tour Manager: 'Never in the history of the sport, at this level, in Australia, has there been an athlete in such great form who exudes such confidence and amazing ability. Owen Wright is a superstar in the making. The scary thing for the rest of the world is that he's only nineteen.'

Dad's reaction? 'Good job. Stay focused.'

STAYING FOCUSED WAS BEYOND me, however. I was more inclined to sit back, breathe in the ocean air, catch up with mates and join them on a trip to the snow. I'd made a lot of money that year. Each Pro Junior win was worth twenty grand; a QS win was worth thirty grand. Inevitably, I started deviating from the program, and relations with my father deteriorated as my results began to slip.

Manly was the final stop on the Pro Junior carousel, which I was determined to clean-sweep even though I arrived on Sydney's northern beaches out of sorts. Of late, I'd been scraping through heats. It was back to burying my face in my hands, crying with a towel over my head and asking, *Why, why, why does surfing suddenly feel so hard again?* To which my father was ready with the familiar retorts: *You've slipped off track. You haven't been disciplined.* And I'd had to admit that he was right. Once I'd done that, the big brain-broom went to work again, clearing the clutter caused by conflicting objectives. I won Manly.

Afterwards, back on the road with Dad at the wheel, me beside him, he said he had something important to tell me.

'There are a lot of talented surfers out there, Owen, but there are very few great competitors. There are a lot of surfers who aspire to great things, but very few willing to make the necessary sacrifices.'

'Yes,' I said. And, at last, I understood.

My father had his way, his method. For a teenager, it was devilishly hard to stick to. But there was no doubting anymore that it worked, or that committing to it half-heartedly would not. My father had been right all along.

12

IN OCTOBER 2009, I went head-to-head for a second time with Kelly, this time at Portugal's aptly named Supertubos, a stretch of sand that produces one of the heaviest tubes in Europe. Dad was there, along with 10,000 spectators on a packed beach.

I'd been walking the line for months and felt unshakeable as I faced off against the king in a Round 3 heat. I knew the calibre of my rival, but this time there was a hint of mutual respect in the air. Kelly started aggressively and stayed that way, leading until the final minutes when I hooked into a long, left-hand barrel, exited cleanly and tossed in an aerial. The upstart had prevailed again, ending Kelly's run towards a tenth world title. It felt like everyone on the beach went nuts. Everyone except me (and my father, of course), because I was a different beast by then, able to feel pleased without going overboard.

I faced the Californian Dane Reynolds in my next heat, which we contested in the big and barrelling conditions we both relished, and he posted two high scores and looked safe until I unveiled a 9+ ride and sent him packing.

That win pushed me into a quarterfinal with yet another American, big-wave specialist and fellow goofy footer Damien Hobgood. The way I was feeling, in combination with the giant surf that day, meant this contest could prove to be the making of me or a disaster. In the end, it was both.

Conditions were a treacherous blend of heavy and shallow, with monstrous waves breaking in thigh-deep water. I took off on one that seemed borderline unmakeable but held my nerve for a 10-point ride in a classic case of high risk, high reward. I was a wildcard competing in a quarterfinal of a tour event and I'd notched a perfect score. My confidence was orbiting Jupiter. Pride before a fall? You got it.

On my next wave I took off fractionally late and dropped like a brick to the seafloor. I must have blacked out because the next thing I knew, I was washing up on the shore like a piece of driftwood. I opened my eyes to see a worried-looking photographer hovering over me. I stood up and tried walking around, but the world didn't look right – it was blurred and tilted.

My father and the ASP medical team arrived at my side. I think it was one of the medicos who confiscated my board because I was making stupid noises about heading back out to defend my lead with fifteen minutes left. The medicos helped me onto the back of a beach buggy and drove me to the medical tent. From there, my next stop was hospital because I had blood seeping from my right ear and severe pain in my neck and right shoulder. Tests revealed a perforated eardrum, a bulging disc in my neck and a subluxated shoulder.

The kicker to this story is that I showed up the next day, ready to compete. It turned out that Hobgood hadn't overhauled my score during what remained of the previous day's heat, and as a result I'd qualified for the semis. So, on a few hours' sleep, with tape wrapped around my forehead,

Rambo-style, I fronted up ready to go. As it turned out, an ASP doctor examined me and ruled me unfit to compete, but that was because of my neck injury not because I'd been knocked senseless the day before. Go home, I was effectively told. Give your ear, neck and shoulder time to heal, then jump back into the nearest raging surf.

In the world of surfing at the time, concussion didn't exist.

FOR THREE MONTHS AFTERWARDS, I wasn't a patch on the surfer I'd been pre-Supertubos, yet neither I nor anyone else could say why.

In the gym, I'd need to lie down on the floor for twenty-minute stretches. My balance was off, which was ruining my surfing and forced me to withdraw from the year's final two QS events. My sleep was shot, and I was as moody as a lovesick adolescent.

Knowing what I know now, it's obvious I had swelling on the brain. But I was trying to live and train as though everything should be as it was. In the surf, I just kept launching and falling, all the while wondering what was wrong with me. My neck and shoulder felt fine, and my eardrum should have healed, so why was I surfing like a novice?

Sometime during all this, my mother did take me to a local doctor. I rattled off my symptoms to him.

'Let's get you a blood test,' he said. 'Could be a virus.'

The blood test revealed nothing of note. But what I'd needed was a neurological exam.

13

'COULD WE ALL SIT down for a few minutes,' my father said, one evening at the start of 2010.

Uh-oh, I thought. The last time Dad had summoned us like that, he'd dropped the bombshell that we were leaving Culburra. Worse, he seemed different this time – graver. Without saying a word, Kirby, Tyler, Mikey and I took our seats around the dining table.

'Your mum hasn't been feeling the best lately,' Dad said.

I shot a look at Mum, who was sitting next to my father smiling weakly.

'She's had some tests and it turns out she has a growth on her brain. It's a tumour but it's non-cancerous.'

I disconnected at that point. I was aware that my father was still talking, but I'd stopped listening. Dad was right: Mum had been complaining of headaches for a few weeks now. Also, everyday mishaps – the spilt milks of life – were bothering her more than usual. But she's very good at hiding pain, my mum; very good at setting her jaw and soldiering on. I hadn't suspected anything was amiss.

I snapped back to the present when I heard Mum's voice. 'It's okay,' she was saying. 'Everything's going to be okay.'

Kirby, Tyler and Mikey were crying. Mikey looked like I felt – spaced out, uncomprehending. We took turns hugging

Mum, who repeated to each of us – kind of whispering in our ears – that she was going to be fine and not to worry.

I was the only kid who wasn't crying but I was scared. I went into overdrive. 'Yes, yes,' I said to Mum, a little too frantically, 'you're going to be fine.'

What I realised later, once I was thinking straight, was that my parents had been sitting on this news for some time, weeks probably. They only told us about it once they had a plan for treatment, which was surgery within the next couple of months.

Being benign, Mum's tumour wasn't going to migrate and it was relatively slow growing, but by this stage it was the size of a golf ball and affecting her hearing. It needed to be excised. I learned that even benign tumours can be dangerous to the point of life-threatening, if they're allowed to expand willy-nilly and press on the surrounding structures of the brain.

IN THE MEANTIME, LIFE – the surfing life I shared with my father – rolled on. I was in the big leagues now and the associated pressure caught me off guard. It probably shouldn't have, but it did.

The tour opener in February was the Quiksilver Pro Gold Coast at Snapper Rocks. It was very much my home break considering how close this rocky outcrop is to the unit I'd shared with Tim. In the lead-up, I did the bulk of my training at Lennox Head, but a couple of weeks before showtime, with my father's blessing, I moved back into the Coolangatta unit to reacquaint myself with the nuances of Snapper.

Unfortunately, I was too accessible during that fortnight. Day and night, friends and acquaintances kept dropping in. All the well-wishing was nice but, combined with the media interest in my debut, the effect was draining. I surfed that event with a cluttered mind and was beaten in Round 3, smoked by fellow Aussie Taj Burrow. A few weeks later at Bells, I was sent packing at the same stage.

Between Bells and the next stop in Santa Catarina, Brazil, Mum travelled to Sydney with my father for her operation. It went okay except – and it was a big except – she was now deaf in her left ear.

A day or two after the surgery, I came down to Sydney to visit Mum in hospital. Her bed was tilted so she was half sitting up, and her head was bandaged. Behind her was a large window through which sunlight poured in, backlighting Mum and offering visitors a view of the city skyline.

She was weak and couldn't turn her head easily, but she turned enough to watch me come in and managed a smile.

Aunty Linda was by her side. I call her Aunty Linda but she's not really my aunt – she's Mum's best friend. My dad was there, too, standing back from the bed. It was very quiet. Mum couldn't talk much but she held my hand when she noticed my eyes were moist.

I was supposed to fly to Brazil the very next day. I was packed and ready to go, but didn't feel right about it.

'Mum, I don't want to go to this next event. I need to be here.'

But Mum shook her head and found her voice.

'No, no. Go follow your dreams. I'll be right here. I'm okay. I'm being looked after.'

But my own travel plans weren't the main issue. In recent days, my father had been intimating that he'd be coming with me to Brazil. Now, here at the hospital, with Mum in a post-operative fog, he confirmed that this was his plan.

I was so angry it was all I could do to look at him. *Weird. Wrong.* Those were the thoughts ricocheting around in my head. Dad and I left Mum and Aunty Linda, and faced off in the corridor.

'What the fuck, Dad?'

'You need me.'

'No, Mum needs you.'

But he was never going to change his mind. My father pretty much never changed his mind about anything.

LOOK, I'M NOT GOING to say Dad didn't make himself useful in Brazil. He handled all manner of necessities effortlessly that would have put me in a sweat. I'd never been to Brazil before. I had no idea where to stay or how to get around; I had no local connections. I could have made those connections, but that would have taken time and energy. I was just out of the juniors competing with men in a strange land, feeling my way. My father took care of everything. In that sense, absolutely, he was a godsend.

More than that, for a lot of the time, we got on great. Both of us were wired to wake around dawn, when we'd hit the road to track down Santa Catarina's best breaks and surf together for hours. Dad would use one of my spare boards, and we'd swap boards from time to time. It was a solid relationship rendered suddenly precarious by this new and large crack.

Among the good times, we had numerous arguments about Dad being there. Aside from my escape to Coolangatta, this was perhaps the first time I'd stood firm in an ongoing dispute with my father. No matter how many times he told me that Mum was all right and in good hands, I wouldn't let up on him.

Another consideration in this was Mikey, who was thirteen at the time. While his mother recovered in hospital from brain surgery, where was his dad? Following me to South America for a surfing competition.

From memory, my father had put Tim in charge while we were gone. Tim would have done his best, but he was twenty-two years old and feeling his way in life. Mikey: the way the cards fell for him, that kid had to learn how to fend for himself. It's no wonder that, nowadays, he can do virtually everything: reassemble a car, fix a leaking roof, plant a garden – you name it. His resourcefulness is exceptional because he had to get used to doing things for himself.

My father did call home during our fortnight away, but only a few times. Calling home was never a strong point of my father's, particularly from overseas at a time when making international calls wasn't as straightforward as it is now. Remember, too, that his first choice always was to live on a shoestring, so calling home a lot seemed like an extravagance to my father.

Somehow, despite the tension, I performed well. After negotiating the early rounds, I beat Jeremy Flores of France in Round 4 and Taylor Knox of the USA in my quarterfinal, setting up a semifinal with Kelly. Dad phoned Mum after my quarterfinal win and put the call on loudspeaker. Mum congratulated me and insisted she was doing well. By that stage, I think she might have left hospital and gone to stay with her parents in Currarong, which is where she did most of her convalescing. Though Kelly beat me in the semis, Brazil was still important for me. By going deep, I'd proven to myself that I belonged in this company, that I could do more than make up the numbers, this year and beyond.

We came home to find Mum on the mend. In my father's mind, her recovery would have been a vindication of his going to Brazil, but I didn't see it that way. Something had changed in the dynamics of our relationship. To me, our disagreement had occurred at a level that went not just to priorities but to values. His choice in this case was never going to be something I could put behind me easily.

What, I asked myself, *was at the root of his decision to come with me?* On one level, I think it was a straight-out case of misjudgement, where he took too much notice of his wife's assurances that she was okay – he took those flimsy protestations way too literally. But I also think there was a degree of selfishness at play. My father loved surfing and this – travelling abroad to see his son compete against the best – was what he'd dreamed of for me. Even though it was me out there in the surf, my father had been planning this for a long time. He'd shifted the family from Culburra to bring me closer to the action. He'd also retired from his work, and it was clear he saw coaching me, managing me and guiding me as his job.

My mind lingered on our arguments in Brazil, where I kept telling him, 'You've fucked up,' or 'This is a major screw-up.' I didn't hold back. I don't know exactly how he felt about copping it from his son the way he did. It's possible he had a phobia about illness and hospitals, which he wasn't going to share with me. But I didn't hold back. All the things a father doesn't want to hear from his son, I said them.

14

NOTHING'S SIMPLE, IS IT? I can tell you that my relationship with my father fractured in Brazil and would never be the same again – and that would be true on one level – but it wasn't as though we were suddenly estranged. He was still my father. I still loved him and depended on him. And I wasn't ready to tell him not to travel with me anymore.

It was complicated, as illustrated by something that happened in September that year, when the tour shifted to the Hurley Pro at Lower Trestles in Orange County, California.

That was another strong event for me. In Round 4, I contested a three-man, no-loser heat with Kelly and another American, CJ Hobgood (Damien's twin brother), with the winner going straight to the quarterfinals. At the time, Kelly was in great form and made a ripping start to the heat, as did Hobgood, while I was searching for rhythm in mouth-watering A-frame waves (waves that break both left and right with perfect shape). But at the back end of the heat, I caught alight, notching a 9.63 score and a solid back-up score to win. I ended up losing narrowly to Kelly in the quarters, but my showing at Lower Trestles strengthened my sense of belonging conceived in Brazil.

One morning during the event, my father received a tap on the shoulder from Andy Irons. In the early 2000s, Irons was the closest thing Kelly had to an equal. Irons had it all: looks, charisma, charm – and preternatural talent. He won three consecutive world championships between 2002 and 2004.

For much of his adult life, however, Irons waged a private war against twin demons: bipolar disorder and opioid addiction. When he spoke to Dad and me at Trestles, he'd just returned to the tour after a two-year hiatus, preceded by a period in which his skills had deserted him. Moves that had been second nature to him had seemed out of reach, and he'd been showing his frustration and bewilderment to the world. *Surfer Magazine* had said he was 'coming apart in front of our eyes'.

'Rob,' Andy said to my father, with a genuineness that moved me, 'I love what you're doing here with Owen.'

By this stage, most people around surfing knew about Andy's mental-health issues, if not the extent of them. As the three of us chatted, what came through was that Andy was loving watching this rookie, me, transition smoothly to the pros, and that he was attributing this in no small part to the firm-yet-supportive father I had beside me. It sounded as though Andy was wishing he could have had a similar presence in his life back in the day, that a Rob Wright equivalent was what he'd needed as his own career took flight.

Only six weeks later, Andy died at the age of thirty-two in a Dallas hotel room from what the autopsy said was a combination of a heart attack and 'mixed drug ingestion'. At the time, his wife Lyndie was pregnant with their son Axel, who turned eleven in December 2021.

Dad's fatherly instincts extended to some of the other young guys on tour, particularly the Brazilian Jadson André, who's a couple of months younger than me. Whereas my dad had virtually glued me to a board once I could walk, Jadson's parents, sensitive to the sport's countercultural associations, didn't like him surfing as a boy. An uncle would secretly take him out on the waves.

Throughout 2010, Jadson and I were fighting it out for rookie-of-the-year honours. Unlike me, he'd managed to win a title – at home in Brazil. Always smiling, always seeing the good in people, Jadson gravitated towards my father and me. The three of us would often be talking about surfing and the tour, and these were very honest chats considering Jadson and I were rivals. He'd tell us how he was feeling about things, and Dad would listen to him and offer advice. Dad thought the world of him and so did I. We'd both watch Jadson's heats whenever we could and cheer him on.

'You know, your dad's great,' Jadson said to me in a quiet moment at Trestles – a sentiment he'd echo many times in the years to come. 'I can't tell you how much I appreciate his kindness to me.'

In the circumstances, some sons might have been jealous, but not me. In fact, it was something of a relief that Jadson's presence diffused Dad's laser-like focus on me.

My father was playing at least three roles in my life: dad, mate and coach. Coaches will film their athletes to identify areas for finetuning. I'd often urge my father to bring along his camera to practice sessions and shoot footage that we could pore over later. And sometimes he would. But he was a surfer too, remember, and only sometimes could he resist the lure of a cranking surf.

What a lot of my father's coaching amounted to was leading by example. He'd wake early, prep for a surf and rev me up in the process. He was also a great reader of surf conditions. I'm sure he felt he could help me more in these ways than by bombarding me with lot of technical advice, which wasn't his forte. My father believed that once you're an accomplished surfer, your body knows what do. What determines your level of performance is how you are within yourself. Are you living correctly? Are you content with who you are? Do you believe in yourself?

It was the same with board selection. I'd be fussing over which one to take out until my father would cut in.

'It doesn't matter which board you ride. You'll get it done.'

15

ULTIMATELY, IT WAS INCONSEQUENTIAL what Andy Irons or Jadson thought about my father, or the role he played in my life. What counted was whether our relationship was healthy and functional. And towards the end of my rookie season, it wasn't. Things were breaking down.

Old cracks had reopened and were now more like fissures. The same old arguments, but the combatants were no longer adult and child, or adult and youth, but two men. Both of us were stubborn – me somewhat, my father ridiculously so. I was twenty years old and crisscrossing the globe, holding my own against surfing's best. My capacity for subservience was drifting out to sea on the tide.

On overseas trips, I stayed with my father in cheap lodgings while gradually stepping out more after dark. I was making friends and keen to socialise – nothing outlandish, just some laughter and, sure, a little alcohol and a bedtime later than my father approved of. Always an early-to-bed-early-to-rise kind of guy, he'd turn in at 8.30 pm and preferred me to call it a night then, too – especially if we were in the one room – and often I would. He'd then be up 5 am to do his exercises.

'You want me to be a robot champion,' I snapped at him in Tahiti. 'It's not me.'

'Not a robot,' he said. 'Disciplined.'

'I'm obviously a disappointment to you. I can't do what you expect me to do anymore. *Just leave.*'

'I don't think so.'

'What are you here for?'

'You need me.'

That was typical of our exchanges, which would usually end with me growling in frustration, tugging at my hair and stomping off.

In calmer moments, I'd challenge him all over again about his fixed ideas on waking times and crack-of-dawn exercise, as well as the material in that personal bible of his about resisting temptation in all its forms.

'None of that stuff is going to win me a heat.'

'Can't you see by now? It's all part of it.'

By the time the tour shifted to southwestern France in late September, I decided I wouldn't stay in the same place as Dad anymore. I made my own arrangements. Don't get me wrong: I was grateful to him for having taken care of our travel plans to this point; he was good at them and they were a weight off my mind. But he'd book us into hovels miles from where everyone else was staying. This was no accident, believe me. He knew exactly what he was doing.

Most fathers would probably take the hint when their son starts finding his own quarters, but not mine. He brushed off the insult and continued to tour with me, tagging along when I'd have a bite to eat with Wilko, the kid from Copa I'd surfed against in my first comp. Both Wilko and I made our tour debuts in 2010 and spent a lot of time kicking around together.

In the early evenings, Wilko, Dad and I might eat together, after which Wilko would be itching to kick on. He was quite the socialiser, Wilko, and I envied him. Even when I defied my father and joined my mate for phase two of the evening, I could never relax because of a gnawing sense of guilt around carousing instilled by my father.

Wilko knew my father frustrated me, but never offered advice, never passed judgement, never told me just to shove off the old man. He accepted who I was and the circumstances I was in. Nonetheless, the preconditions for an explosion were set. It happened on the open road.

THE NEXT STOP AFTER Soorts-Hossegor, France – where I was eliminated in Round 4 – was Peniche in Portugal. Dad and I made the 1000-kilometre journey in a rental car. This was a marathon drive through Spain, during which there was little for two guys at loggerheads to do besides bicker.

By this point, I was fed up. Yes, Dad was kind of cramping my style – if I had a style to cramp – but more importantly, the issue of Mum hadn't magically fixed itself. Come October, she was still unwell. She remained in the care of my grandparents in Currarong, where old friends were pitching in, taking her to doctors' appointments, cooking for her and keeping her spirits up. Mum may have been out of danger, but she wasn't out of the woods. There's a long recovery involved when someone drills a hole in your skull to remove a tumour from your brain.

Meanwhile, there were three kids at home in Lennox Head, who needed to be up early every Monday to Friday to get themselves off to school; there was cooking, laundry, home maintenance . . . and all the rest of it. What I'm saying is, my siblings needed a parent, and instead of filling the breach while Mum was down, Dad was in Europe driving me spare.

We were well into our ten-hour road trip to Peniche, the lush green beauty of the Basque Country having dissolved into the desert of central Spain, when the blow-up happened. If the issue of Mum was the bomb, a flare-up over our route lit the fuse.

I had a map open on my lap, but Dad wasn't following my directions. Nor did he seem to be taking any notice of road signs. Eventually, I couldn't contain myself.

'What the fuck are you doing?'

'Relax. It's all right to get lost, you know. It's when you're lost that you learn the most.'

'No, no! We're going to be driving for fucking ever!'

'It'll be an adventure.'

I lost it. I called him every name under the sun. Then he started yelling, too. Dad was turning puce and the veins on his neck looked like pythons. Suddenly, his right hand flew off the steering wheel and crashed into my head. In his fury, he'd backhanded me.

For a few minutes, we sat in silence, both of us staring straight ahead as the desert flashed by. Finally, without looking at him or thinking, I spoke.

'You're done,' I said quietly.

Dad said nothing.

That was a long trip. Very long and very quiet.

In the comp, I bombed out. And then it was time, I knew, to resolve this thing. We were watching a heat from the beach, both of us standing with arms crossed.

'Dad, you need to let go. You've got other kids, you know.'

I glanced over. I'd cut him deeply. As I've said, my father never showed much emotion, but there was a sadness in his eyes you couldn't miss.

'Yep,' he said.

All the tension and fighting had exhausted even him.

It was over.

EXCEPT IT WASN'T. NOT QUITE. We'd had an ugly falling out and for a fortnight or so afterwards, we exchanged barely a word. But then Dad seemed to accept the split. Things improved between us to the extent that I caved in and agreed to give our partnership a swansong of sorts in the year's penultimate event, in Isabela, Puerto Rico. My resolve wavered: 'All right, okay, come to Puerto Rico,' I said. It was partly about making up with him.

In Puerto Rico, I surfed well, expertly at times, before losing to Michel Bourez of Tahiti in Round 5. In December, I went alone to Pipeline, where my run was ended in the quarters by Flores.

My first year on the tour was complete. Despite all the tensions with Dad, and the sadness and worry around Mum, it had been a success. I had an overall seventh-place finish and recognition as Rookie of the Year. In more ways than one, it had been my breakout year.

16

THOUGH DAD WAS OUT of the picture as my coach, I was in no rush to replace him. I figured I'd manage on my own for a while at least. But what was Aristotle's line – nature abhors a vacuum? So it proved in this case.

My body felt battered after my first season on the tour and the after-effects of my wipeout at Supertubos. I wondered aloud one day about the best person to see for treatment. My mother, who was still regaining her strength, reminded me of a local kinesiologist and massage therapist, Dean Davies.

In late 2010, I started having semi-regular sessions with Dean, and we got to talking. He'd been an elite 800-metre runner, just shy of Olympic standard; more recently, he was an age-group world champion in downhill mountain biking. He could surf but he wasn't a surfer. To my mind, there are surfers and there are people who try to surf but aren't surfers. Dean didn't claim to be an expert in surfing, either in theory or practice.

His treatments seemed to help: my body – my back especially – felt looser, which was exciting because in sport, body maintenance is half the battle. If you're hurting, if your movement's restricted, if you're harbouring doubts about your body's capacity to withstand what you're about to subject it to, you have no chance of performing optimally, irrespective of how brave, skilful or experienced you might be. Another plus for Dean was his expertise in the psychology of sports performance. He believed variations in performance could mostly be explained by internal forces. Feelings of calm and confidence, he told me, were precursors to high-quality performance, while agitation, uncertainty and diffidence were preconditions for failure.

'Surf in the moment,' he urged. 'Be impervious to distracting thoughts.'

At the time, this was all new to me and I lapped it up. Lately, I'd become conscious of an emerging barrier in my futile quest for surfing perfection. As a boy, I'd surfed with abandon. But the knockout at Supertubos had given me pause. Insidiously, a kernel of fear – or perhaps caution – had crept into my work. Subtle though it was, I'd started to hold back.

As a practitioner of applied kinesiology, Dean believed the muscles can provide biofeedback on where there may be blockages of energy in the body. Left unresolved, he said, these blockages could undermine performance and increase feelings of stress and anxiety. Dean said he could correct these imbalances and relieve them. *This is freakin' great*, I thought.

Even though Dean was treating my aches and pains, and tweaking my mindset, it hadn't occurred to me to bring him on as my coach because he wasn't a surfer. But one day, he surprised me with a question.

'What more do you actually need from a support person?'

'Well, mainly just someone to film me,' I said.

He could do that, Dean replied.

The venue for the 2011 tour opener was Snapper Rocks, just an hour or so away for both of us. That appeared to get Dean thinking.

'Why don't I come up and treat you during the event?'

'Okay,' I said. *Why not?*

So, Dean was with me at Snapper, treating me on competition days and lay days (when competition is suspended due to poor surf). I had a passable event, knocked out in Round 3 by rookie Alejo Muniz of Brazil. Dean and I repeated the arrangement in April at Bells, where I paid him for his time, plus extra to compensate for being interstate and unable to see his regular clients.

From there, before the next stop in Brazil, we started discussing Dean joining me on every stop on the tour. From my standpoint, I was glad to be getting some relief from the bodily pain that had become a constant companion. As for Dean, my guess is he liked the idea of travelling the world while working with a pro surfer. On top of that, I'm sure he thought it would be good for his business.

I could have gone either way on this one. It's not like I needed Dean. But in the end, I green-lit a fulltime professional relationship. Dean came onboard as my travelling coach – or, more accurately, my non-coaching coach, because he couldn't and didn't offer technical advice. Nonetheless, the way we both saw it was that he could still improve my surfing by knocking my body into shape by various means. We settled on the title 'performance consultant' to describe his role.

Our relationship would not end well. But I'll get to that.

*

ALSO IN 2011, I regained a foothold on the South Coast. After crashing for multiple spells in the Thirroul granny flat of a friend of mine, the highly successful and influential board shaper Phil Byrne (no relation to Laurie, though they worked together), I bought a townhouse in Thirroul. It was just around the corner from the granny flat and one block back from the beach. That place was hard to damage when I hosted a party because it was decked out in dark-brown carpet that concealed virtually any mishap. When I wasn't touring, I spent most of my time living alone in my new place, while catching up with some old buddies who still lived on the South Coast – Keegan, Ty, Stephen Kelly (Stevo, a great mate from schooldays) and Parrish Byrne (Laurie's son).

It was a great area for surfing, too. I spent a lot of time at McCauley's Beach, a little stretch between Thirroul and Bulli with a terrific right-hand break. Most waves on the tour are right-handers. I happen to prefer left, but what can you do? I tested a lot of boards in that period. By then, I disagreed with my father that you could ride an ironing board to a world title if you trusted in yourself. I was determined to have better equipment.

I was still seeing Dad on visits to Lennox Head. He was sceptical of Dean's credentials and feeling a little bruised that I'd replaced him, Dad, my own flesh and blood, with . . . *a kinesiologist?*

While he didn't like it, to his credit, he pretty much held his tongue – around me, anyway. My father isn't the kind of person who seeks to bring others down. It's one of his best qualities.

17

THIS SEEMS LIKE A good time to tell you a little more about Tyler. If my life has been a rollercoaster, so has hers.

Through childhood and adolescence, while I stepped in and out of my dad's champion-building program, Tyler didn't. She was always in, always committed to the hilt. And while I had lots of friends and relished spending time with them, in and out of the water, Tyler was more introverted. She skipped the breakout phase that temporarily ripped my family and me asunder.

Success came quicker for Tyler than it did for me. She was fourteen when she became the youngest surfer to win an ASP World Tour event – the Beachley Classic at Manly in October 2008. In 2011, at the age of sixteen, she was fulltime on the tour with our father watching out for her. From where I was standing, it always looked like Tyler was going to be better than me. Mikey, too. They both seemed more gifted.

A quick digression. Mikey: oh man, he was unbelievable as a kid. His appetite for big surf, for what surfers call charging, was insatiable. There was no hesitation with Mikey. No fear. This one time, he and my father were at Redsands in Shellharbour on the South Coast. Redsands is a reef break that you access by jumping off the rocks. Waves lurch onto this little shelf and barrel and spit; there are urchins and barnacles underneath. Like Aussie Pipe, you shouldn't go near Redsands unless you're an experienced surfer, but Mikey took no notice of that kind of baloney. That day, Koby Abberton was in the surf being towed onto waves by a jet ski. Meanwhile, my father was pushing Mikey onto the same monsters –Mikey was nine at the time.

Anyway, back to Tyler. Things happened fast for her. So fast that before she knew it, she'd swapped her childhood for professionalism and all that goes with it: the merry-go-round of training and travelling, winning and losing.

The tour challenged her – and it was challenging for me to watch her. I tried to be the older brother, bringing her into my friendship group like Tim had ushered me into his. One time, we were in France. She had a quarterfinal in about half an hour, and she was still in slumberland because she'd mis-set her alarm or something. I woke her up, chucked her stuff in the car and drove her down to the beach. She ended up winning the whole shebang, but she only just made it to that round.

When my father stopped being my coach at the end of 2010, you might have assumed that he'd have shifted his focus onto Tyler and become her travelling mentor. But that didn't happen. By that stage, the combination of his eccentric ways and controversial choices had strained his relationships with all my siblings. As a result, I became something of a link between him and them.

'Look, he's not that bad, guys,' I'd say. 'He's okay. He means well.' That sort of thing.

But Dad and Tyler were never going to join forces in 2011. It was too late for that. Dad had spread himself too thin for too long. In the fatherly attention stakes, for no good reason, I'd fared much better than my sister.

Did my father place a higher priority on my success than Tyler's? It's a good question. I think the answer is 'yes'. I'm sure Tyler thinks the answer is 'yes'. Exactly what my father's thoughts were on equal treatment, I can't be sure. My feeling is the discrepancy wasn't a matter of male chauvinism, but more a case of him feeling a special attachment to me and my quest, for unknown reasons. Because Mikey missed out too, of course. My father too often assumed that the baby of the family would be okay without his dad around.

Dad did a lot of things right. In many respects, he went above and beyond as a father. I think his plan to raise champions was noble, if imperfectly executed. Looking back now as a father myself, I feel for him. He had three children bursting with surfing talent, as well as two other children to worry about. He bent over backwards for us kids. He didn't drink; he didn't smoke. He was this wholehearted bloke and family man, who took us camping, watched all our sport, coached our soccer and footy teams, and ran Nippers. Those paternal responsibilities piled on top of his marriage, his business and his own passion for surfing meant that he was, as I said, overstretched. Something had to give. In the end, it was the relationships he held dearest.

18

IN SEPTEMBER 2011, I landed in the Big Apple for the Quik-silver Pro New York. I'd come via the heavy waves of Teahupo'o in Tahiti, where Kelly had edged me in the final.

While happy with how I was surfing, I wasn't hopeful about my prospects in this event. The forecast for Long Island was for puny surf, never my preference. Typically, the smaller, lighter guys excel in those conditions.

New York was dangling the first million-dollar purse in surfing history, including US$300,000 for the winner. These facts were plastered everywhere and the surfers were abuzz. It was enough to quicken the pulse and tighten the muscles. Yet for me, the forecast had a counterbalancing effect: believing I had no chance of winning, I felt unusually calm.

Then fate stepped in. On the eve of the event, hurricane Lee formed over the Gulf of Mexico. It came ashore over Louisiana and kept moving northward, eventually joining a frontal system and soaking and buffeting the eastern USA. Lee caused thousands of evacuations and extensive damage to homes, and took a handful of lives. All of which was terrible. But from a position of pure self-interest, it also whipped up the kind of swell I see in my dreams, turning Long Beach into a mouth-watering left-hand break.

I surfed the way I'd always pictured myself surfing: smoothly and powerfully, while sticking a highlight reel of spectacular airs. Other guys were relishing the conditions, too, but I kept winning my heats and with every victory grew in confidence. I'd entered that mystical place where you're not thinking, worrying or analysing, but simply releasing the talent you have inside you.

I made it all the way to the final on a day of four-foot barrels. Once again, my opponent was Kelly, whom just about everyone expected to win. My strategy was simple: take the first wave, post a score and cast Kelly in the role of chaser. Everything went to plan. I started with a 7+ score, then conjured a 9.23 and later an 8.67. Kelly was Kelly, but even he couldn't overhaul my imposing total and eventually broke his board trying.

For the first time as a pro, I'd won. And I'd picked a fine event at which to break through.

Between drying off and the presentations, my phone pinged with messages. One was from Dad: 'Well done,' it said. 'Great to see you doing your thing.'

On the podium, I was buzzing. 'Thanks to my coach, Dean Davies,' I told the throng. 'To my dad, I wish he were here, but another day.'

I let my hair down after that, hanging out with mates for four or five days and nights in New York, not returning during that time to the hotel where Dean and I were staying. There was some drinking in nightclubs, but nothing excessive. Mainly, we acted like tourists, checking out the view from atop the Empire State Building, attending a Yankees game, strolling through Central Park. I had a great time. But Dean was displeased. Like my father, he seemed opposed to the concepts of celebration and decompression. My recollection is that he was calling around, telling anyone who'd listen that he couldn't reach me, that I'd left him in the lurch. When I finally returned to the hotel, he let me have it.

'Where the fuck have you been? I've been sitting here twiddling my thumbs for five days.'

I gave him short shrift. His attitude was a troubling echo for me, and an alarm bell. It was one thing for my father to have ruled with an iron fist; it was another thing entirely for Dean to be acting like my keeper.

If Dean thought that, by taking a break, I was burning my chances at the next stop, I proved him wrong. Arriving in California for the Hurley Pro at Lower Trestles, I felt refreshed. In Round 3, my opponent was surfing's newest hotshot, John John Florence. I was widely tipped to lose because there was a justified sense of 'here-he-is!' about Florence, who was eighteen at the time.

I woke up that morning in a friend's place at San Clemente feeling unusually anxious. Dean tried to calm me by having me do breathing exercises and stretching, but none of it was helping. I became short with him.

'This is shit,' I said. 'It doesn't work.'

'Shut the fuck up,' Dean snapped. 'Put your fucking shoes on, and let's go outside.'

I ignored him for a while, but he was insistent. 'You want to be ready for this fucking heat? Then follow me.'

We walked for a bit until we came to the bottom of a hill. 'Okay, we're going to run up this thing,' Dean said. 'Let's go.'

As we were running side by side, I started grinning and scoffing because this felt pointless. Suddenly, Dean's arm shot up and caught me on the side of my scone. Then he did it again. And again. I was having to raise my arm as a shield.

Soon, we settled into the task of running up this damn hill. We did it seven times, gradually ramping up the speed until we were all but sprinting. When we stopped, we were both doubled over, blowing hard. Then we walked to a spot where you could see the ocean.

'Okay, take a look out there, Owen. This is your office,' Dean said. 'You've spent more time in the water than you have on land. You know how the ocean works more intimately than anything else. Take ownership of that. This is your day to step forward and do what you've been training to do all your life.'

Hours later, I came from behind to defeat Florence in a high-scoring heat: 17.84 to 17.13. With a few minutes left and needing a 9-point score to advance, I locked into a long right-hander and unloaded a series of ferocious backhand blasts to notch a 9.77.

'John John's got a massive future ahead of him,' I told reporters afterwards. 'But I had a bit more to drive for with the world title on the line and it pulled me through. It wasn't just a Round 3 heat for me out there.'

That evening, I turned to Dean. 'I know I wasn't appreciative at the time, but thank you very much for what you did.'

Sometime later, I came across the science behind the hill running – and Dean's twitchy arm. Turns out, you can't be anxious and exhausted at the same time. The running and whacking were part of what's called a 'pattern interrupt' – an unexpected stimulus that jolts you into a different state of mind.

I kept winning, and in the final Kelly and I squared off again. Never in tour history had the same two guys contested three straight deciders. For one magical month, the ASP World Tour had become the Slater and Wright Show. 'There were aerials, slob grabs, 360s, crazy cutbacks, intense roundhouses and breathless floaters for every taste,' *Surfer Today* said of the final, which Kelly won. As usual, he was a gracious winner. He told the media there were no weak points in my surfing, that I'd be a threat everywhere I went.

I finished third that year. Not bad. Kelly won again, claiming his eleventh world title. It was also his last, though as I write this, he's still competing. On 11 February 2022, he turned fifty. Six days earlier, he won at Pipeline. What can I say about Kelly Slater that hasn't already been said? Probably nothing, but I'll say this: we will never see his like again. His personality, his style of surfing and his approach to life are all unique. Collectively, they've changed – and continue to change – the face of our sport.

JUST BEFORE CHRISTMAS 2011, Dean's role evolved to include taking charge of my physical training. The way he'd talked about fitness had long intrigued me. He explained how he'd trained in his running days, how regimented his approach had been. As someone steeped in discipline, I was fascinated.

While Dean and I came from different worlds, that was far from being a deterrent. I liked the idea of experimenting with alternative methods. I was no stranger to hard training, but what I hadn't done was break down surfing into its constituent parts and target each in isolation. I'd regarded surfing as a form of training in and of itself, but Dean urged me to rethink that notion.

'No, no – you surf at this time, you train at this time.'

Just before Christmas 2011, he offered to take ownership of my fitness and map everything out.

'Okay,' I said. 'Let's give it a go.'

My new routine entailed several paddling sessions a week on Lake Ainsworth in Lennox Head. When you think of surfing, you probably picture a dude upright on a board, riding a wave. And fair enough. But getting on that wave in exactly the right place at precisely the right moment involves paddling, often at a rapid clip. Striving to up my paddling speed made sense. And Dean and I were both committed to the goal; not once did we cancel a session for inclement weather. In pouring rain and howling winds, we'd be out there on Lake Ainsworth first thing, me going all out prostrate on my board, with Dean perched on his stand-up paddleboard yelling encouragement and timing me.

I also did up to four weights sessions a week in a public gym, with Dean by my side for maybe half of them. The aim was to build strength and muscle, to encase my joints in an armour that would protect them against the rigours of surfing.

Dean had identified an imbalance in my upper body: I was much stronger through my back than my chest. You could hang weights plates from my waist and I'd do wide-grip chin-ups until the cows came home, but my bench-press was schoolboy stuff. So we focused on correcting that imbalance – and on my legs. With a supportive belt cinched at my waist, I performed set after set of squats and deadlifts using very heavy weights. I'd done resistance training before but never like this. As an approach to fitness, it was a radical change for me and unorthodox in surfing at the time.

Again, though, it made sense. Surfing starts in the legs, with balance and stability on the board. Strong thighs lower your centre of gravity, allowing you to maintain that classic surfing stance against the buffeting of the waves. The stronger the better, I figured.

Rounding out my new regimen was a weekly stair-running session targeting my aerobic base. You can snatch a heat with a 9-point ride at the death, like I did against Florence, provided you have energy left in the tank. You never want to squander a chance because you ran out of puff, not unless sleepless nights are your thing.

19

IN EARLY 2012, I went to Bali with some mates – Stevo, Parrish and Keegan – for a surfing holiday. One day, out of the blue, my father showed up, materialising in the cheap and cheerful hotel we were staying in.

'Dude,' I said, shaking my head. 'What are you doing here?'

Dad said he'd come to hang out with us.

That disappearance was the last straw for my mother. When Dad arrived home a week or so later, she was gone. She'd packed her bags and left.

Mum called to tell me what she'd done.

'All right,' I mumbled. Because what was I going to say? That Dad didn't deserve this? That she was being unreasonable?

When she'd needed him, my father wasn't there for her. Only Dad failed to see that. He had co-raised his children to independence and then, mission accomplished, forgotten to refocus on his wife. It was a monumental blunder, which cost him his marriage.

Only after Mum left did my father realise how much his absences had hurt her. But while guilt and regret kicked in, he was too proud to grovel. He was too proud to throw himself at her feet, plead for forgiveness and vow to do better. If he'd done that – and I begged him to – that would have worked, I think. Mum would have come around. But he didn't.

Their split cut me to the quick. Until shortly before it happened, the idea that they might part one day had been inconceivable. I figured that life throws problems at couples and you fix them in response; you don't burn down the house. I thought of my parents as two great people, and that remains my opinion to this day. Nothing's worth a bust-up, but I wasn't going to argue with my mother because I knew that my father's inattentiveness in her hour of greatest need was indefensible.

Shattered, Dad would turn to me in the weeks and months afterwards. And every time he'd raise Mum, I'd tell him the truth.

'Mate, you made a mistake, and you didn't go back and fix it. You didn't grovel. You're coming to me upset, but you didn't take that on board.'

Dad would look gloomy and distant and slowly nod his head.

My mother left Lennox Head and returned to the South Coast – the region she knew as home – renting a house in Gerringong. Mikey chose to live with Mum. With Tim long gone, and Tyler and I travelling constantly (Tyler with Kirby as her chaperone), that left Dad alone, rattling around in the big house in Lennox Head into which he'd moved his family only two years earlier.

Wherever I was competing, he'd call me at all hours. We'd have these wrenching conversations that might last ten minutes or half an hour. Even though he'd brought this catastrophe on himself, I felt sorry for him.

'I still love your mother,' he said. 'I will always love her. I got married and she's the person I married, and I will never look at another woman.'

He meant it, too. There has never been anyone new – neither for him nor Mum.

AMID MUM AND DAD'S separation, I was never going to set the waves alight, especially since other stuff was going on that was dimming my spirit.

After sixth months' training under Dean, I felt burnt out. I'd trained too hard for too long with insufficient rest, while seeing less and less of my friends. I'd worked out six days per week and stacked on ten kilograms of muscle. I was as heavy as I'd ever been – about ninety-two kilograms. I was lifting some big loads, like 130 kilograms for squats. I hurt my back doing those at the start of the year. But I'll say this: I was ripped. If you'd asked me whether I'd ever looked better, more muscular, I'd have said 'no'. Socially and mentally, my newly conspicuous physicality was working for me. But it was another question entirely whether the extra bulk was helping me in the surf. I didn't think it was.

'What are you doing, man?' That's what a lot of people were asking, as they eyed my bulging muscles that were forever threatening to shred the clothes I was wearing, Hulk-style.

'Yeah, you're big, man,' I was hearing, 'but you're not your usual zippy self out there.'

They were right. I'd slowed down. I'd lost confidence in my ability to perform aerials. I was carrying too much weight.

It was good weight, in the sense that it wasn't fat, but it was weight nonetheless. Because I was a surfer and not a body-builder or sumo wrestler, it was an encumbrance. To be fair to Dean, our principal goal had been to increase my strength, not my size. But there was no denying that a by-product of the training had been some quite prodigious muscular growth.

Dean was losing me. While I never doubted that he wanted the best for me, he was too intense, too analytical, for me. I felt he was too intent on attributing my every loss, my every missed wave, my every botched turn to some deeply buried psychological issue. I could accept that there may have been some value in discussing certain issues I'd had with my father over the years, and even perhaps some subconscious desire of mine to win his approval through surfing. But I felt Dean went further. I sensed he wanted me to change the dynamics of our father–son relationship, to put more distance between my father and me – and between some of my mates and me.

In the middle of 2012, word reached me that he'd told some of my mates to stay away from events because their presence was distracting me. While Dean denied this, I was in no mood for a debate.

'You've got me so wrong,' I said. 'I'm not in the same head-space as you are.'

Later, I thanked him for his help . . . and terminated our relationship.

AFTER TWO AND A HALF years on the tour, I was jaded, phys-ically and psychologically. This got me thinking about Tyler:

if I was feeling deadened, how must she be feeling? Since her breakout win at fourteen, the pressure of pro surfing was all she'd known, and Tyler lacked the network of friends that I could lean on and relax with. She had Kirby, and Kirby was priceless but a big sister can do only so much. We were all dealing with our parents' bust-up. And Dean had been in Tyler's ear, too.

Lately, Tyler had been struggling in the water, surfing without her usual passion and generally seeming miserable. I knew I had to see her and talk to her. Something was wrong.

In July, Tyler, Kirby and I were all in California. On a whim, I drove to the hotel near Huntington Beach where my sisters were staying in the lead-up to the US Open of Surfing, the final event on the women's circuit.

I found Tyler in a dark place, emotionally. She was lying supine on the bed, hands behind her head. I sat down near the footboard. Kirby was sitting on the other side. She was down in the dumps, too.

Things kicked off with a kind of communal weep. Lately, there hadn't been nearly enough contact between either of my sisters and me, and we all knew it. Then I plunged in.

'You may not want to talk about this,' I said, looking at Tyler. 'That's okay. I'll talk, you listen. Something's not right here. You've lost your spark. I need you to know, *you don't have to do this*. You're eighteen years old. You don't have to have a career in professional surfing. From the outside, it looks like we have this great life of surfing and international travel. But we both know how hard it can be, and I think I know how you're feeling.'

Tyler looked at me with an expression of surprise and gratitude. Ever since she'd won that pro event at fourteen, she said, she'd been chasing wins all over the world. The sport that used to give her joy had become a source of unrelenting pressure.

'The thing is,' she murmured, 'I don't know whether I want to do this anymore.'

That was okay, I told her. It was okay to feel that way.

Then I told her I wouldn't be seeing Dean anymore, that I'd cut him from my team.

Tyler found her voice in that conversation. She let go of some of the things that had been weighing on her. Shortly afterwards, she began a six-month break from surfing – not just competitive surfing but all surfing. She said she needed time away, she needed to wind down so she could think about who she was and what she wanted.

My sister and I have never had a more important conversation. It was the first time we'd spoken like adults and in the spirit of emotional care. For once, no one said anything about waves or boards or manoeuvres. There was no surface-level banter. We talked about Mum and Dad busting, and how crazy-driven we'd been our whole lives. We spoke like grown-ups, instead of shallow kids.

'We've been so hellbent on getting to where we are now,' Tyler said, 'that neither of us has ever taken a breather. We've never popped our heads up to see what else there is around. We've had this very narrow life experience.'

I gambled that day, showing up and saying what I did. It could have backfired, because who wants to be told they're flaming out? Fortunately, Tyler had been ready for a brotherly intervention.

UNLIKE TYLER, I KEPT surfing in 2012, but I decided to take a more laidback approach. That meant a lot less training, being answerable to no one, and having more fun.

It wasn't coincidence that, getting about in that new frame of mind, I started seeing someone, who for the purposes of this story I'll call Hannah. We met one weeknight in a bar popular with students from the University of Wollongong. After we'd been together for a while, I invited her to come along to the late-season tour events, which took us to the USA and Europe.

Having Hannah with me shook up my approach to the time between comps. Where in the past I'd treated them as opportunities for practice and training, now I saw them as free time in which to accrue some non-surfing memories. Hannah was keen on making the most of being abroad, and I was equally keen to do anything besides train my arse off. With no coach hassling me to 'dig deep' or 'push through the pain', we did as we pleased. My father and Mikey joined us in Europe. Loving being back in the inner circle, Dad was shrewd enough to keep his counsel on all matters surfing, training and diet.

It was around then that a physical trainer checked me out.

'Man, you've trained your body into oblivion,' he said.

I wasn't the fiercest of competitors for much of 2012, but I did all right, finishing tenth overall. More important than my ranking was having backed off, mentally and physically.

For one of the few times in my life, I'd chosen to be my own best friend.

In December, I could reflect on the year and smile. I'd connected with my sisters, and travelled like a tourist instead of an athlete. There's a big difference, believe me.

20

SHIT! SMASH. BLACKNESS.

One mid-morning in March 2013, shortly after the tour opener at Snapper Rocks had been surfed and won (by Kelly), I was driving in Tweed Heads South in a supercharged V8 utility courtesy of Ford, one of my sponsors.

I was a bit of a revhead at the time, not a complete lunatic but a bit stupid, I guess. As I rounded a roundabout, I slid out, and instead of easing my foot onto the brake pedal, I jammed it down on the accelerator. The ute went careening into three roadside trees, which snapped and came crashing down on the roof and bonnet. The windscreen cracked, the airbags inflated, and I was knocked unconscious. For how long, I don't know, probably a minute or two.

When I came to, I barely knew which way was up.

I got out and tried in vain to shove the trees off the bonnet. Some passers-by helped push the ute off the road.

I called my father, who'd driven up from Lennox Head for Snapper. He was on the scene in a flash, beating the police and the towie. The cops recognised me, and they were cool. They had to fine me for negligent driving, though.

No one said to me: *Get yourself in front of a doctor, son. You were knocked out. That's serious. You need to be checked out.*

No one said it – and it didn't occur to me to take myself off to a medical centre or the nearest emergency department. In fact, I was more concerned about my right ankle than my head. It felt banged up, though not so badly that I wanted it examined. You see how the mistakes are mounting up? I've just suffered another concussion and ignored it.

That was the end of that ute, by the way. Shamefaced, I had to go to Ford and say, 'Er, sorry, I've written off your car.' It was embarrassing – I felt like a cliché. But they took it well and, not long after, they were kind enough to give me the keys to an SUV.

Next stop on the tour was Bells Beach. My mate Parrish came along with me. A couple of years older than me, Parrish had been on the QS with me. He gave it a red-hot go but missed out on qualifying, even though he was a tremendous surfer. Ultimately, he retired from fulltime competition to devote himself to shaping.

In the lead-up to Bells, I was noticing strange fluctuations in my emotions. My sleep was also a mess, as was my surfing. I spent hours in the water trying out boards – Parrish had brought along more than twenty – and felt ungainly on every one of them. My balance was off and the power had left my surfing.

'Man, I just cannot link anything together,' I said to Parrish after one particularly dispiriting session. 'I'm just so off.'

Parrish's focus was the boards and he searched for an explanation in them. But the problem wasn't in the boards; it was in my head – in my brain – only I didn't know it.

In my Round 1 heat against the Hawaiian Dusty Payne, I wiped out on my first wave, landing awkwardly as it broke on

Dad, my older brother Timmy and I in 1990, the year I was born. We are in the shed we lived in before Dad built our home on the beach.

Looking cool!

Grinners are winners!

My cousin Brooke and I playing dress ups. She's still one of my best friends.

Riding motorbikes on the neighbour's block, age 6.

My 7th birthday
with Dad.

Primary school swimming carnival. I'm in the middle, with Keegan to the left and
little Mikey off to the side.

Surfing Aussie pipe to train for Indonesia.

Me (front) and Timmy to the right at Uluwatu on one of the first trips. Dad's on the left.

Sand boarding.

Uluwatu Temple on
a family holiday to
Indonesia.

Family photo after
they all moved to
Lennox Head. Right
to left: Kirby, me,
Mum, Dad, Mikey
and Tyler.

Kita and I in Yosemite when we first met.

Coming out of a second 10-point barrel in Fiji in 2015. Photo by Kirstin Scholtz, World Surf League/Getty Images

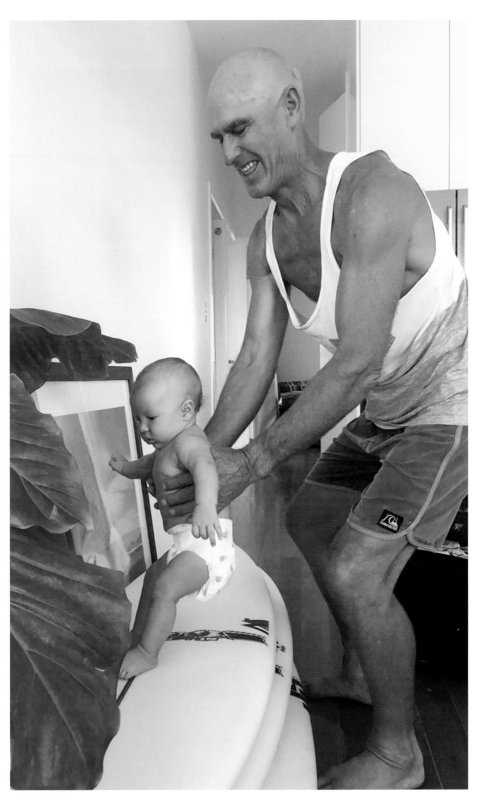

My dad with my son in 2017, before Dad's diagnosis.

Right after I won Snapper Rocks coming back from the head injury. Kita and I celebrated where we'd come from. Photo by Kelly Cestari, World Surf League/ Getty Images

Gabriel Medina and I at Teahupo'o in 2019. This victory sealed my Olympic qualification and marked the first time since the accident I felt like the competitor I used to be. Photo by Matt Dunbar, World Surf League/Getty Images

Proposing to Kita in Tahiti in 2019.

The last event my dad ever made it to in 2019. Photo by Gerry Nicholls

Our wedding in the hills behind the Gold Coast, 31 January 2020.
Photo by Lucie Blake Photography

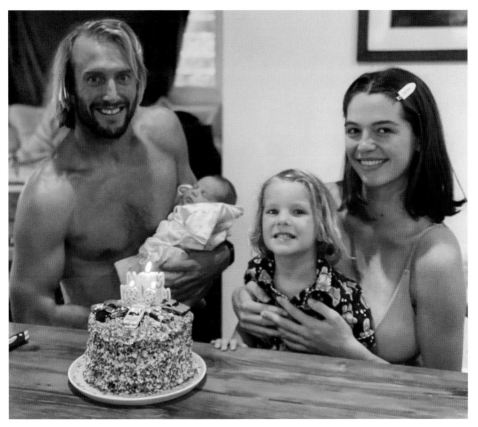

My birthday . . . the day after Rumi was born.

Rumi and I down at
the river on a family
camping trip.

Winning bronze at the Olympics in 2021. Photo by Ryan Pierse, Getty Images Sport

Family photo with my mum after the Olympics.

For my 33rd birthday, Kita gifted me my jersey from the New York contest I won in 2011.

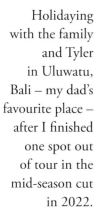

Holidaying with the family and Tyler in Uluwatu, Bali – my dad's favourite place – after I finished one spot out of tour in the mid-season cut in 2022.

Jill and Laurie Byrne. Laurie shaped my first ever custom surfboard and was my first mentor in surfing.

After my last competitive heat at Bells in April 2023. Everybody is wearing T-shirts with my name and career highlights. Photo by Beatriz Ryder, World Surf League/Getty Images

top of me. A jolt of pain shot down the back of my right leg. I kept surfing but couldn't score more than a 2. Back on land, the pain, now centred in my lower back, was severe. Hannah helped to extract me from my wetsuit and get me dressed. My right leg wasn't working properly. I was struggling to lift it off the ground and take a step.

I went back to my place in Wollongong, where for two days and nights, I struggled to climb in and out of bed. On the third day, scans revealed damage to two discs in my lumbar spine. There was an annular tear at L5/S1 and a seven-millimetre bulge at L4/L5. Clearly, I'd be missing a bunch of events. The only question was how many.

Backs heal slowly. No one can massage a disc back to rubbery good health. Doctors floated the idea of surgery. 'No thanks,' I said. For weeks, I confined my treatment to core and breathing exercises. Then my own research led me to a local Corrective Holistic Exercise Kinesiology (CHEK) practitioner who – as per the CHEK system – was determined to treat me holistically.

'Okay,' he said, 'mentally and emotionally, where are you at? Let's address this full circle.'

While I indulged him a little in those areas, his focus soon shifted to the corporeal. I was carrying a lot of bulky muscle, he noted.

'Let's strengthen the little core muscles underneath,' he said. The implication was that I'd built a mansion on shaky foundations.

He started me on a program of super-basic exercises, such as lying on my stomach and arching my back slightly. I committed to it, attacking the exercises three times every day.

My back started to improve. Had the program worked? Or had time and the body's own healing mechanism weaved their magic? I didn't know. The point was, I could imagine surfing again. I set myself the goal of competing in the Fiji Pro in early June.

AT THAT STAGE, I still didn't realise that I'd had a head injury, that certain lingering symptoms were neurological relics of the concussion I'd suffered in the car crash. The worst of these was insomnia. In bed, I'd shut my eyes and begin to drift off, then some malign force would shock me awake. You know that feeling, yeah? It's like when you're about to nod off and you dream you've tripped over or fallen down some stairs, and you snap awake. Except I wasn't dreaming, and this would happen ten times or more a night. It was distressing. And by day, it could reduce me to a shambling wreck.

I googled away and soon figured I must have sleep apnoea. I spent a night in a sleep clinic hooked up to machines but nothing conclusive came of that.

'You're not sleeping, so your back isn't healing as fast as it otherwise might and you're feeling burnt out. That's probably why you're moody,' my CHEK practitioner said.

While this was all logical, it still missed the point; it missed the obvious, which was that I had a head injury.

In time, I crept back into the water. I surfed a few times and started bringing more energy to the gym. I was connecting with my friends and feeling better, but I was still tired, man. So tired.

Fiji was closing in. I felt I'd done enough right in rehab to resume my place on the tour. I'd certainly spent out the wazoo on medicos. But then, in the surf at Shoalhaven Heads one morning, I had another setback. I paddled into this wave and went up for a floater. On top of the lip, it was as though a sniper had nailed me. The wave dropped suddenly, as though the floor had disappeared from beneath my feet, and I plunged like a stone, taking another wipeout. My right leg got stuck underneath me, and I felt the same shooting pain as before.

I had more scans, the results of which hit me like a punch in the chest: the annular tear at L5/S1 was now a disc herniation. This is where the nucleus of the disc pushes through a crack in its casing, irritating nerves in the spinal canal and causing pain and numbness. In my case, I had a reduced sense of feeling on the outside of my right foot.

Fuck it, I thought. I wasn't going to keep putting pressure on myself to make it back to the tour. I decided to write off the rest of the year. Just walk away. This wasn't a papercut I was dealing with, after all. I could still avoid surgery, probably, but I needed to give the injury time to heal.

But you don't stop thinking, do you? You don't stop looking for answers. Maybe these wipeouts were happening because I wasn't sleeping right. I underwent more sleep assessments, which all but ruled out apnoea but couldn't tell me what was wrong. I figured I had nothing to lose so I acquired a sleep-apnoea machine and connected myself to it at home.

It didn't help because apnoea wasn't the issue. My airways weren't closing; they were fine. (What was happening, I know now, was that my brain was trying to protect itself. Detecting the loss of sensory perception in the act of falling asleep, the concussed brain can interpret this as an emergency. When that happens, its default response is to shock you awake. I'll tell you more about that later.)

I couldn't solve the mystery of what was happening to me and – more surprisingly – neither could the people I was seeing.

What should I have been doing? Resting. Staying home and relaxing, asking as little of myself as possible. There's not a whole lot you can do to accelerate your recovery from a severe concussion, but there is a whole lot you *shouldn't* do. And in my ignorance, I was doing what I shouldn't.

21

FROM MY ANGLE, I had one job and one job only: to get back on tour in tip-top shape as fast as possible. As well as the drive to be surfing and competing again, your finances loom large when you're beached. The public thinks: *Oh well, he's injured but he'll be right – he'll be back soon.* But that's not necessarily how your sponsors see things. They're more likely to be going: *Where are you? You're not being seen by millions, so where's the return on our investment? And where were you in the pecking order when you pulled out, anyway? Were you setting the world on fire even before you got hurt?*

Rip Curl were understanding, but I still had to reshape our contract and take a hit, which was fair without being a fillip.

Looking to accelerate my recovery, I thanked my CHEK trainer and shook hands with a guy named Aaron McKenzie, a movement and lifestyle coach in his mid-thirties, who was operating a fitness studio and health-food café in Sydney's eastern suburbs. Aaron had many high-profile clients, including big-wave surfer Mark Mathews and the champion National Rugby League (NRL) players Anthony Minichiello, who'd suffered terribly from lower-back pain in the latter half of his playing days, and David Williams, known widely as 'Wolfman' because of his untamed hair and beard. After showing up unannounced at his studio one weekday afternoon, I liked Aaron immediately. He was warm and welcoming, and I could soon tell from the way he spoke and carried himself that, in matters of diet and fitness, he knew his stuff backwards.

And boy, did he look the part! He was one of those people known in fitness circles as a weapon or a beast. He believed in stretching and warming up everything, not just the hamstrings and quadriceps but wrists, fingers and ankles. As flexible as a yogi, he could manoeuvre his body into all manner of unthinkable poses, and lift weights from positions that most people wouldn't dream of lifting weights from. Nutrition fascinated him. He had firm views on the subject, which contrasted sharply with my father's. For Aaron, there was no question I should be eating meat. Meat, as one element of an entirely wholefoods diet, was the ticket to rude health, he believed.

I'd never met a more can-do person. He asked me about my injuries. I recounted what I thought of as the gruesome tale of my lumbar spine.

'Okay,' he said, as though I'd just told him I'd stubbed my toe last week. 'And what is it you want to achieve?'

'I want to get back to the tour.'

'No. Nup. What do you want to do *once you're back*?'

'Well, I want to be winning again.'

'No. Nup. Think bigger. Think higher. Where's surfing going next?'

'Well, it's moving into aerials. Guys are probably going to start doing flips soon.'

'Okay,' he said, leaning back in his chair, a smile creasing his face. 'That's where we're going.'

In that first exchange, Aaron changed how I viewed my circumstances, zapping all traces of self-pity and spiking my expectations. Where I'd wanted merely to escape my prison of pain and surf again, he saw grander possibilities.

'You're going to come back,' he said, 'and you're going to reshape surfing.'

'Well, shit,' I said, sitting straighter, my eyes aflame. 'I mean, all right!'

Let me background you (very briefly) on the aerial revolution that was brewing at the time. In the 1970s, Hawaiian surfer Larry 'The Rubberman' Bertlemann started to release his fins from the wave's face during his top turns. Later, as surfboards became more manoeuvrable, aerial pioneers such as Matt Archbold, Christian Fletcher and Jason Collins took matters up a notch. Given the symbiotic relationship between surfing and skateboarding, it was inevitable that surfing's finest would soon be performing gymnastic feats that had once been confined to surfing comic-book fantasy. Anyone aspiring to surfing greatness was on notice: they'd need to conquer the air.

Why not me?

Aaron's words were inspiring. *Wow*, I thought. *This guy's not the least concerned about my back.* Everyone else had been concerned. Studying the X-rays or listening to me describe the damage to my discs, their brows would furrow. They'd be cautious and noncommittal in predicting the course and duration of my recovery. I'd been picking up a vibe of: *Hmmm, this poor sap might never be the same again.*

By contrast, Aaron was looking around the gym going, 'You see that guy? He was way worse than you. Look at him now!'

In his early twenties, while doing capoeira – a Brazilian martial art that involves acrobatics – Aaron had suffered severe neck and shoulder damage, which put him in often severe pain for six months. But now, he was lifting weights using only his neck muscles. He was downplaying my injury and I liked that. I was ready for that. He exuded a positivity that lifted my spirits.

Aaron and I got into a routine where I'd do a training session with him around the middle of the day, then we'd sit down together at his café for lunch. Over fruit-and-vegetable smoothies or slow-cooked beef sourced from local farms committed to regenerative agriculture, we forged a friend-ship built on shared interests and (I felt) a shared energy or spirit.

'Who's been your major influence on diet?' I asked him one day.

'A guy by the name of Weston A Price.'

I gave him a quizzical look.

'He was a Canadian dentist, born around 1870, I think,' Aaron said. 'He travelled the world in the early days of commer-cial flight, studying traditional cultures. He wanted to know why all these people had perfect teeth and big, broad smiles, while guys like us from, if you like, the "civilised world" had all these dental deformities and cavities.'

'Interesting.'

'Yeah. He found that the common thread among all the cultures with robust health is a traditional diet, usually based on animal food. But just as important as what they eat is what they *don't* eat. No refined grains – white rice, white sugar, white flour. No canola oil, soybean oil.'

'I love it,' I said. 'My dad raised us to avoid processed junk. But it's tough on the road, you know? What are you supposed to do when you're travelling?'

'It's harder. But don't think of it is as trying to be perfect. Just stick as much as you can to wholefoods.'

At another lunch, after I'd been training with him for a few weeks, Aaron got onto the topic of impregnability – of training in ways that protect you from just about anything your sport can throw at you.

'Take me, for example,' he said. 'Before I injured myself, the conditioning I'd been doing wasn't sufficient for what I was asking my body to do in capoeira. The whole point of training is to condition yourself above the demands of what you're doing. In your case, we need to make your body as strong as possible, so it can handle whatever you ask of it in the ocean and so your back is never an issue again. We need to condition you to be able to twist and turn in all different directions, so you can have an extreme level of body awareness or proprioception. Then, your challenge will be to take that ability and apply it to your surfing.'

I remember I said something self-effacing, to the effect that I couldn't imagine doing a lot of the strength-and-balance moves that Aaron made look easy.

'No, listen,' he said. 'You're one of the most talented athletes I've worked with in terms of your ability to pick things up quickly. Things it took me ten years to master, you're mastering in a couple of sessions. You're going to overtake me before long.'

'Thanks,' I said, 'but I don't need to tell you that a lot of what I'm doing hurts. Sometimes, I think I'd be better off resting, giving my body time to heal.'

'Wrong headspace,' he said. 'You're too focused on getting rid of the pain. I want you to focus on getting stronger so the pain will no longer be part of your experience. The injury is still going to be there but if you're strong enough *around* it, it won't matter. You can sit back and wait for injuries to heal, but while you're doing that, you're getting weaker and weaker, and mentally you're going downhill.'

Aaron had trained a lot of surfers over the years and seemed to understand us. The way he spoke about surfers' connection with their environment, you'd have sworn he'd spent countless hours out the back, waiting for something juicy to loom on the horizon.

'You're all very connected with nature because you're in it, and your performance or self-expression depends on being able to read the surf,' he said. 'There is a strong connection with a traditional way of life, with peoples who never saw themselves as separate from nature but as belonging to it.'

At Aaron's, I advanced from doing not much to lengthy weights sessions and gymnastics-style training, including somer-saulting off a trampoline. There was pain at every stage but, in time, I not only healed but was as strong and injury-proof as I'd ever felt. The round trip from Wollongong to Aaron's fitness centre in Bondi Junction took three hours. It was a slog, but I did it four or five times a week because I was determined to get myself right.

A casualty of this singlemindedness was my relationship with Hannah. I was so focused on my rehab, she couldn't have felt other than of secondary importance to me. I was also moody and sleep-deprived – less-than-great company, basically.

In the end, I started renting a place at Bondi Beach to be nearer to Aaron's, and Hannah and I fell out after eighteen months together. While the ending was untidy, it didn't change the fact we'd had fun together, or that she'd helped to show me there was a world beyond the waves.

22

REPAIRED AND REFRESHED, I began the 2014 tour with a new coach, a former pro surfer I'd known for years. When I was a teenager getting wildcards into tour events, Matt Griggs was co-coaching the pro Rip Curl team. I'd made several trips with him, including to Bali and Tahiti, and found him a great guy to be around. Although he was a bit of a legend and I was still just a teenager, he was pumped with me because I was keen to surf the bigger waves – to have a crack. He would hold me up to the pros and say, 'Look at this kid out there . . . what are you characters doing?'

Matt steered Mick Fanning, his great mate, to his first world title in 2007. At the end of 2008, Matt left tour-level coaching and took to meditating in the Royal National Park near his home in southern Sydney, at a time when a lot of people associated meditation with cultists in orange robes. Matt felt he'd been living the lives of his charges more than his own, and wanted to explore life's meaning and possibilities beyond the subworld of re-entries and cutbacks.

In late 2013, we'd bumped into each other at a grommets' surfing clinic and got to talking. Nothing happened immediately, but over two or three conversations, we began to see the appeal of an alliance. Matt told me that when he thought about the two of us, he had a sense of unfinished business.

The decisive chat occurred over lunch one day at a café in Thirroul.

'I saw something in you as a kid, but I skipped out before you qualified for the tour,' Matt said. 'Look, I've been happy off the pro scene. I've no desire to go back. But there's something in you that I see as unique. I feel you're a world-title contender. You've got me curious.'

I was curious, too.

'Let's do a few one-on-one sessions and see how it feels,' Matt suggested.

I agreed. And from there, it was a short hop to a fully-fledged coach–athlete partnership.

Matt subscribed to something called Kelee Meditation. The word 'Kelee' has its roots in 3000-year-old Sanskrit. Understand 'the Kelee', Matt told me, and you can silence the hum of negative thoughts that undermine your talent.

'Think of the Kelee as a receptacle,' he said. 'You can take bad things out of it and put good things in.'

'How?'

'Through meditating twice a day. Stay with it, and you'll start to develop a mind that is open to everything but affected by nothing.'

At Matt's urging, I started meditating and journaling every morning and night. The journaling complemented the meditation. Both were ways to target my shortcomings. I'd sit still with a problem, and see what thoughts and feelings I had. I discovered they were mostly turbulent – there was a lot of frustration and confusion stemming from my injuries, my parents' break-up, pressure from sponsors and being off the tour.

So, I now had Aaron in Sydney guiding me on nutrition and fitness, and Matt in my corner providing mental and spiritual support. In Matt, for the first time, I also had a coach who knew surfing inside out: the technical side, board science, wave knowledge, tactics – the works.

Together, Matt and I watched countless hours of footage of champion surfers in action, studying their body positions for different turns. He helped me to develop a frontside carve (which would soon help deliver one of my best wins on tour). He showed me which turns tended to score highest on various types of waves, invariably backing up his advice with statistics – more stats than I thought possible for one man to collate. He could tell me, for example, my win percentage when I caught the first wave of a heat (it was comfortably over fifty). In short, Matt analysed surfing at a level of detail I'd never known before.

This is awesome, I thought.

But as my team was falling into place, an issue was brewing with my equipment that was about to drive a wedge between a mate and me.

Although I'd been using Byrne boards since I was five, that was no reason to keep using them if they weren't my best option, Matt reasoned. 'We're going to cast the net wide and start again.'

In the lead-up to the tour opener at Snapper, I tested about fifty boards. Ten or twelve of them were Byrne boards, another twenty-five were JS Industries and the rest were Mayhems.

At Snapper, the Byrne boards weren't working for me. Try as I might, I couldn't extract what I needed from them in terms of responsiveness. On the beach one morning, the time had come to initiate a god-awful conversation with Parrish.

I'd known the Byrne family all my life. I'd grown up around the corner from them. More recently, I'd lived with them. Parrish's dad Phil was like a second father to me; Parrish like a brother. But with a heavy heart, I broke it to him that from now on I'd be sourcing my boards from someone else.

'I have to do what's best for my career,' I said.

I switched to JS Industries, a board-making giant head-quartered on the Gold Coast. With the advent of machine shaping, JS could knock out about fifty boards for me in a couple of weeks. Matt and I decided to go all in with JS, so I'd turn up at every event knowing I'd be using their boards, rather than going through a process of experimentation with two or more makes of board before every competition.

Explaining this to Parrish and the Byrne family was always going to be hard and made worse by my avoidance of the subject. They had invested untold time and emotion into my surfing. None the less, off I went. There was hurt. I was just as upset, and I also felt guilty. It took a while for our strained relationship to come back to what it was.

My best result that year was at Jeffreys Bay, South Africa, where two next-gen goofy footers, Wilko and I, contested the semifinals against two veteran regular footers, Mick Fanning and Joel Parkinson. Mick and I were all business; Joel and Wilko were relaxed. The older guys, who were great buddies, handed Wilko and me a pair of hidings. They then proceeded to put on a masterclass in the final, a high-scoring exhibition of otherworldly surfing. To this day, I rate it as the best final I've seen. Ultimately, Mick prevailed, zipping around on a shorter board.

The following year in the same waters, with Mick defending his title in the final against Jules, a great white appeared beside him. How did he escape that encounter unscathed? Take your pick between quick thinking by Mick (who lashed out with his fists and feet) and pure good fortune. People ask me whether I think about sharks when I'm in the water. The answer is 'no'. Never. You can't. The day you start, you're finished.

Coincidentally, less than an hour before Mick's brush with death, Wilko and I had been on a Rip Curl trip elsewhere in South African waters. I watched from the boat as these incredibly powerful creatures smashed into the sides of a cage and obliterated the baits. I could have been *inside* the cage but, frankly, I didn't want sharks associating me with food.

Disembarking the boat, we were watching the final on our phones. We saw the shark pop up next to Mick, then both disappeared behind a wave. At that point, you could only fear the worst.

That evening, I rang my mother. Like everyone who'd seen what happened, she was unnerved.

'Please come home,' she said.

Wilko and I both wanted to do just that, but we had to stay and fulfil our Rip Curl obligations. We skirted around the edges of surfing, though. We either stayed out of the water altogether, or else surfed terrible waves when there were lots of people in the water.

From J-Bay it was on to Teahupo'o, a village on the south-west coast of Tahiti that's home to one of the world's most perilous breaks. An extremely shallow coral reef produces large, hollow, left-breaking waves that bend and race before closing out onto dry reef. Just my thing, really.

At Teahupo'o, I was charging as hard as anyone and reached the semis, where I took a wipeout against Medina. I was concussed again – I know that now – but at the time I paddled back out and took off on another ten-footer. I was not examined by a doctor. I lost to Medina.

Later that year, just for fun, my coach Matt and I decided to visit a fishing hamlet in Portugal called Nazaré.

23

LOCATED ON THE CENTRAL coast of Portugal, Nazaré was a sleepy little place until 2010, when Garrett McNamara paid a visit. A local had written to the big-wave surfer from Hawaii, urging him to check out the monstrous swell that occurred off Nazaré each year between March and November.

Typically, giant waves happen when moving water goes from very deep to very shallow waters over a short distance. Off Nazaré, an undersea abyss runs from 225 kilometres out to sea right up to Praia do Norte (North Beach) and then stops. At points, it's 4.8 kilometres deep, three times the depth of the Grand Canyon.

From the lighthouse overlooking Praia do Norte, McNamara watched slack-jawed as sets of waves rolled in. After telling loved ones he'd stumbled upon the holy grail of surfing, he soon after made Nazaré his second home. In 2011, at the age of forty-four, he rode a wave measured at seventy-eight feet. And ever since he set that world record, Nazaré has been a magnet for the world's most daring big-wave thrill-seekers – and legions of gawkers.

In 2014, Matt suggested we visit Nazaré after the tour event in Peniche, sixty or so kilometres to the south. He didn't imagine us getting towed into monsters or anything ridiculous;

he simply wanted us to see the swell with our own eyes and perhaps surf some smaller waves nearby. Looking ahead, Matt regarded me as someone capable of winning at the bigger-wave venues, including Pipe and Teahupo'o. Any exposure to larger surf would be worthwhile, he figured.

We arrived in Nazaré and stood atop the cliff overlooking the ocean. The waves weren't touching seventy-eight feet that day – they were maybe half that – but still they were bigger than any I'd seen before.

Garrett was the only surfer in the water. I'd have been mad to join him, but I liked watching him at work. *One day,* I thought, *when my competition days are over, maybe I'll become a big-wave guy.* They're a different breed these people – crazy-brave – but not so different from competition surfers that some of us can't imagine having a crack at what they do.

About 300 metres to the right of where Garrett was operating, there was a section of ocean offering smaller waves. Smaller, but still big and thick at about twelve feet. These were tempting. Pointing seaward, I looked at Matt.

'What do you think? I reckon it looks doable.'

Matt grimaced. 'I don't know if you'll get out, man.'

'I reckon I will.'

So, out I went. As usual, when in the thick of it, the waves were more imposing than they'd looked from land. Each time one approached, I felt like a pea before a waterfall. Still, I got three or four decent barrels. Matt liked what he was seeing and paddled out, too. By then, I was pumped up and itching to take on something larger.

When you've spent as much time in the ocean as I have, you learn to read it. I sensed something tantalising on the way and was all but rubbing my hands together. Then, suddenly, a mountain of water veered over from Garrett country. I swear it blocked out the sun before crashing down on top of me.

Maybe fifteen seconds after impact, I surfaced, dazed and confused, to find my leg rope snapped and my board in pieces. I'd been pushed way out the back. The safety of shore looked impossibly distant.

Panicking was one option. But I stayed calm enough to allow years of childhood experience in surf lifesaving and tri-athlon races to kick in. First, I waited, buying time for my head to clear and my breathing to normalise. Second, I exploited a rip to pull me sideways and then towards shore. Third, I body-surfed an eight-foot wave and ate up another thirty metres. That wave deposited me back in the impact zone, but at least I was going in the right direction.

Still out of my depth, I bobbed around in fast-moving whitewash, spreading my arms and letting the ocean effec-tively spit me out. Finally, I felt sand beneath my feet.

I stood on the beach and looked out to sea. I could see Matt, who clearly had no clue I'd been in strife. I could also see fragments of my board.

Later, in the carpark, I was getting changed when Garrett pulled up beside me in a red vehicle and spoke to me through the open window. We knew each other a little from Hawaii, where the McNamaras are a famous surfing family.

'I saw you out there,' I told Garrett. 'I surfed out the front here. I just got obliterated.'

Garrett's eyes widened, but he didn't reply right away. It was as though he needed a few seconds to compute what I'd said.

'You surfed out here? Where's your rescue team?'

'Oh, I didn't have one.'

'Did you wear a vest?'

'No, I didn't have one with me.'

By this stage, Garrett was kind of shaking his head. 'So, you surfed by yourself? No precautions?'

It felt like I was being scolded, which I was, probably justifiably, but I wasn't in the mood for it. 'Yeah, I did surf it by myself,' I said.

Matt joined us then, and Garrett said, 'You guys are stupid.'

'What do you mean?' I said.

'This is the craziest, most dangerous wave in the world. You don't treat it lightly. You shouldn't be paddling out there without a rescue team and a life vest.'

We'd been rebuked. But on reflection, I liked that encounter. Garrett had shown me what a deeper level of respect for the ocean looked like. He exuded it. Yes, he was also in the water among bigger waves, but he had a guy on a jet ski out there with him, and doubtless someone up high as well – his wife Nicole maybe – spotting him.

What I'm saying is, you can be daring but sensible at the same time. You can manage risk. I wish that lesson had sunk in for me before it was too late.

IN THE WEEKS AFTER Nazaré, I didn't feel right. My sleep was shot again, and I felt sluggish. Booked to surf in a couple of

154

QS events in Hawaii before Pipe, I sent a message to the ASP saying I'd be a no-show due to ill-health. Again, I was dealing with post-concussion syndrome but didn't know it.

I still turned up at Pipe to compete, knowing a good result there could give me a top-ten finish for the year. Before competition, I felt exhausted, barely able to get out of bed in the Rip Curl House. I was starting to think I had chronic fatigue syndrome. A doctor visited the house but couldn't find anything wrong with me. Neither of us raised the issue of head knocks.

I battled through a few rounds of competition before taking another wipeout, partially re-dislocating my right shoulder. It was a nasty, debilitating injury that would need time to heal. I was done for the year.

Back home, I stayed with Mum in Gerringong. Nursing my shoulder, sleep-deprived and unable to surf or train, I slid into a mild depression that I attempted to treat with an unfamiliar agent: partying. I went out a lot and got hammered. My new mates thought I was a fun guy. My old mates raised their eyebrows because this wasn't the person they knew – the Owen who rarely drank and forever put his surfing first.

Some of them wanted to talk about my new approach to life.

'I don't know what's going on,' I told them.

24

BETWEEN PIPE AND THE start of the 2015 tour, I decided I'd
try life without a coach for a year. Matt and I hadn't had much
contact. I was probably guilty of not returning his calls when I
was in a post-party funk. Matt was (and is) a very disciplined
and clean-living guy, so I had no expectation of receiving any
sympathy from him. Also, his return to pro coaching had proven
more hectic than he'd imagined – a blur of airports, road trips
and hospitals. In late January, he and his wife Kate welcomed
their second child, Obi, so his focus was now on his family.

Meanwhile, I wasn't training. Because of my shoulder, for
weeks I couldn't paddle let alone surf. Amid all the carousing,
the truth is I wasn't too bothered about the layoff.

'Look, I've loved everything you've done for me,' I told
Matt. 'But I just can't apply myself.'

To the best of my knowledge, it was one of those rare,
mutual, zero-hard-feelings partings.

Life felt strange. My self-image had been built on surfing
and self-discipline; now, I'd disconnected from both.

'I don't know if I'm cut out for this anymore,' I told Mum.
'I'm feeling quite . . . I don't know, something's going wrong.'

We agreed I should avoid making any life-altering decisions while still injured.

The next day, I resolved to lift my game. Step one was getting my body right. I checked in with Aaron, who gave me a basic training program and helped with my shoulder. I'd been sitting around, waiting for it to get better, but it wasn't. Aaron prescribed a shoulder-specific routine – a bunch of band exercises that put the joint through its full range of motion under resistance – that I still use today.

A fortnight out from Snapper, I started to come right. My shoulder hurt less; I was sleeping better; and I felt clearheaded, energetic and ready to go. It was as though I'd emerged from a three-month fog. What I'd do, I decided, was train less but smarter, compete like the devil and then have some fun afterwards. I'd have a few beers at the end of every event, and revel in the fact I was both single and coach-less.

A legacy of my time with Matt was a folder stuffed with technical and tactical pointers matched to each event. There were notes about what had and hadn't worked for me in respect to board and wave selection. Now entering my sixth year on tour, I set myself the goal of winning the world championship. To do that, I'd need to win two or three events. I identified Fiji, Tahiti and Pipe – the big-wave venues – as my best chances. Make a couple of quarters or semis elsewhere, I figured, and I could be number one. I fitted in two trips to Tahiti before Fiji with the aim of making imposing surf feel familiar and manageable.

The tour kicked off with three home legs – Snapper, Bells and Margaret River – where I placed thirteenth, fifth and ninth, respectively. Nothing flash, but something was brewing –

I could feel it. At J-Bay, I made another quarterfinal, where Wilko sent me packing. Next stop: Cloudbreak, Fiji.

Capable of handling rideable swells as high as twenty feet, Cloudbreak is a left-hand reef pass that breaks off Tavarua, a tiny, heart-shaped island lying ten kilometres off the west coast of the main island of Viti Levu. The wave here is off-the-charts frightening if you're off your game, but dangles the promise of the wave of a lifetime if you're well-prepared and daring. In the first half of June 2015, that was me. Actually, I was borderline cocky: *I'm going to do so much damage here*, I was telling myself.

The waves were big – barrelling at eight-to-ten feet – but after my stints in Tahiti, they looked like two-footers. In Round 5, I came up against Adam Melling, a Lennox Head local, and scored a perfect 20 – two 10-point rides – only the seventh recorded in the history of pro surfing. The next day, in the final against Jules, I did it again.

It's a strange beast, the 10-point ride, as elusive as a shooting star. To get a 10, you need everything to line up – board selection, conditions, fitness, form, decision-making, confidence, wave selection, luck – a perfect storm of serendipity. To get four 10s in two days . . . that's a miracle.

As a surfer, you're often miffed and occasionally infuriated by the judges' scoring. Many times, I've mumbled *What the fuck?* when scores seemed to me to be too low for what I or Tyler or whomever I was supporting had just produced. It's a subjective caper. But the funny thing about 10-point rides is that, when they happen, they're as clear as day to everyone who knows anything. You just know: that was a 10. They're rarely disputed.

After the final, I told reporters I couldn't believe what had happened. I'd benefited from smart prep, great boards and studying the best guys at work. I'd been watching the ocean before the final, I said. 'I knew it would turn on. I knew I just I had to be in that rhythm. The waves came and I took them.'

Man, did I feel like celebrating. But with whom? Flying solo – no coach – and with no loved ones having made the trip, there was a distinct shortage of equally enthusiastic would-be revellers on hand.

There was a flight leaving Nadi for Sydney that afternoon, and I took it. Before boarding, I called ahead. Parrish, bless him, would host a party in my honour in his Thirroul shop after closing. I crossed land and sea to get there, coming in the backdoor at about 6 pm to find a roomful of ebullient mates watching a rerun of my final on a gigantic mounted TV screen. The beer flowed and everyone carried on, ribbing me and putting shit on me in the way guys do when earnestness would spoil the mood.

My head didn't the touch the pillow until midnight. Up until that point in my life, I doubt I'd had a better day.

PART TWO OF MY world-title-winning strategy, winning at Teahupo'o, didn't come off though I went close, losing to Medina in the semis. Looking ahead to Pipe, I surfed this wave called Depot Bombie on the South Coast near Gerringong. I went there with a couple of bodyboarders, who were pumped because I was in the race for the title and bound for Pipeline. Producing a not dissimilar wave, Depot is great practice for Pipe.

On this day, the surf was probably fifteen feet, bigger than you'd get at Pipe. These two guys and I were taking it in turns being towed into a wave by a jet ski. I got put on one that was too much to handle and took another wipeout. The world went black. I came to on the back of the ski, with no idea how I'd got there or for how long I'd been underwater or unconscious. But by now, I was so used to getting knocked out and soldiering on that I told the boys to deposit me on the next wave. I wasn't done yet. *Let's go.*

I slept at Mum's that night. When I woke up the next morning, it was all I could do to get out of bed and plonk myself at the breakfast table.

'I feel like a ten-storey building has landed on me,' I said to Mum.

'What do you mean?'

'This is way worse than any hangover I've ever had. I don't know what's going on.'

It shouldn't have been a mystery, I realise. You're probably wondering why I was so slow on the uptake. *You've been knocked out cold, sunshine. You've been concussed. The sensations you're having are symptoms of that concussion. Keep ignoring them, keep getting smashed and you're inviting them into your life.*

And fair enough. But I was oblivious to all this. The only explanation I can give you is that, at that stage, the dangers of concussion hadn't permeated into surfing. Footballers faced them. Boxers. But not surfers. Getting cleaned up by a wave . . . that's different from being hit by a swinging arm or a fist, isn't it? And hadn't my dad told me never to succumb to fear, to tell the ocean who's boss?

I felt terrible for two weeks. Exhausted. I didn't leave the house once in all that time. I figured maybe I'd just been worn out by an eventful year.

'I feel like I've been hit by a bus,' I told Mum.

She told me later that I'd said that to her about twenty times.

25

IN SEPTEMBER 2015, KITA entered my life. I was in southwestern France, staying in a house with Tyler in the lead-up to our respective events. I'd posted a photo of an awkward-looking wipeout (not involving me) on my Instagram account. Kita, whom I didn't know, 'liked' the photo and commented on it. I clicked on her profile, scoped her out and saw we had quite a few mutual friends. She turned out to be Nikkita Alexander, an Australian singer-songwriter who'd released her debut single a couple of months earlier – a song I knew. So I followed her and commented on a video of her mimicking a dolphin call – a warbly, high-pitched screech that I thought was hilarious. Then she DMed me a photo of a polar bear. We were off and running.

Sometimes, little stuff happens that you sense isn't so little. Since I'd made the tour, a lot of girls had posted comments on my feed. This felt different. So, I did a little digging.

'Oh, yeah,' someone told me. 'She's good friends with Nick Pollet.' Nick was Wilko's videographer (and a mate of mine, too).

Originally from Brisbane, Kita was currently living and working in London, writing and recording. Lately, she'd started watching surfing on television. She'd been feeling homesick, she said, and surfing reminded her of home in a soothing way.

She was no expert, though. She said the only surfers she'd recognise if she bumped into them on the street would be superstars like Kelly and Mick. Sorry about that, she said.

I asked Nick Pollet, 'What's she like?'

'Oh, she's really cool,' he said. 'I think you'll like her. She's super-tall, for one thing.'

I spoke to Wilko, too. 'Yeah, she's rad,' he said.

It was crazy. I was excited to be in touch with this girl, so excited I had butterflies. I was like a teenager again, and like teenagers do, I asked for help with what to say. We were bouncing off each other, usually late at night, and I wanted to keep the momentum going, not bring it to a standstill with an ill-considered remark.

I'd be like: 'Tyler, look at this. What should I write here?' Or: 'Tyler, what do you reckon about this?'

'Yeah, that's pretty good,' she would say.

Tyler was laughing at me occasionally because I was so worked up, but it was good-natured laughter. And she'd advise me, not tease me. She's one of those supportive people, Tyler.

For weeks, Kita and I exchanged messages. We seemed to be on the same wavelength. She sent me a couple of her song drafts to check out. Finally, we arranged to meet in Sydney in November. For me, this would be between the second-last event of the year in Portugal, and the final in Pipe. Our plan was to have breakfast at Porch & Parlour café in North Bondi, followed by a bushwalk.

As the day neared, I called Keegan. As kids, Keegan and I surfed and kicked around together on land. As well as being next-door neighbours, we went to the same primary and high schools, and we both did surf lifesaving. To this day, ours has always been one of those effortless friendships between two likeminded guys who never try to be anything except ourselves in each other's company. While our paths diverged in terms of career – Keegan went into building and construction – our bond has never weakened.

'What have I done, man?' I said to Keegan. 'What was I thinking? I'm going on a *morning date!*'

Breakfast had seemed like a good idea at the time – you know, casual, chilled – but the more I thought about it, the dumber it appeared, because it took the option of having one or two loosening drinks out of the frame.

'You'll be fine,' Keegan said. 'You're just nervous.'

I was also thinking, *I must have been tripping to have suggested a bushwalk afterwards.* I'd wanted to come up with something different – from her Insta profile and messages, Kita seemed a little unorthodox – but that brainwave of mine was beginning to feel like a wrong move.

I arrived at the café first and waited out front for her. It was a Wednesday from memory, about nine o'clock. A minute or two later, I saw her walking towards me. What a sight! She was certainly tall, like Nick had said, and she had masses of brown hair that cascaded down to her lower back. She owned her height, holding herself upright, and she moved easily, gracefully. She flowed. When she saw me, her face lit up. She was gorgeous. *Wow*, I thought, *this girl is like a super-confident rockstar mermaid.*

I can't remember much of what we talked about in the café.
I do remember liking her hat, which was leather with a cowgirl
vibe.

'I really like your hat.'

'Thanks,' she said. 'It's my farm hat.'

I also remember saying how I was jet-lagged, a condition
she knew all too well. It probably wasn't an earth-shattering
conversation, but it all felt natural even though I was nervous,
and I think she may have been too, a little.

After breakfast, I drove us to the Royal National Park,
south of Sydney. It took an hour or so. On the way, Kita told
me she'd never been south of Cronulla. Because of all the road
trips I'd done as a surfer, I knew my way around. It was easy to
give the impression of being a man in control, which is a nice
way to feel on a first date.

Inside the park, we blazed our own trail up an embank-
ment to a large, platform-like rock from which we looked out
over Hacking River. We sat there. For a while, neither of us
said anything. You might think silence on a date is a bad sign,
but it wasn't – it was the opposite. We were relaxed enough in
each other's company not to feel the need to fill every second
with chatter. We absorbed the view and the peace.

'Wanna have a swim?' she said.

'Sure.'

We found this waterhole encircled by the rockface. We'd
both come prepared for a dip. As it turned out, Kita had just
got a tattoo inked onto the underside of her left forearm – a
dolphin/shark hybrid. She wasn't supposed to get it wet it for a
while, so she was swimming on her right side with her left arm

outstretched above the water. I thought that was nice. I also liked how she didn't mind stripping down and getting wet on our first date. She was comfortable in her own skin and had every reason to be.

We drove back to Bondi. That was our date as far as we'd planned it, but we were both happy and hungry, so we grabbed some lunch.

Between mouthfuls, Kita said, 'I've got this thing to go to tonight.'

'Cool. I was going to catch up with some friends in Bondi tonight,' I said. I was seeing Ty and his wife Lil.

'Yeah, some friends and I were probably going to have a few drinks around here,' she said.

I felt like she was giving me an opening to jump through, so I said, 'Should *we* have a few drinks?'

'Yeah. We should.'

Phew. Good outcome – because I'd found out earlier that I wouldn't be seeing her again for a while. The next day, she was flying to Los Angeles for work.

After lunch, we parted and did our own thing for a few hours. I went and trained with Aaron up the road in Bondi Junction, while Kita had to shoot a promo for a radio station – a little acting gig that featured a dog.

THAT NIGHT, WE SLOTTED into a group of her friends and mine for dinner and drinks in Bondi. It was a newly formed combination of ten or so people but, as far as I could tell, everyone was happy.

Then Kita happened to say how old she was. She wasn't talking to me at the time, but I heard her say, 'Oh yeah, I'm nineteen and . . .'

I almost choked on my beer. *Nineteen?* I was twenty-five.

I swear you'd never have picked her as a teenager. I'd been chatting with her (electronically, admittedly) for a month and a half, and nothing about her conversation suggested adolescence. Then, having spent the day with her, bushwalking and sitting on that rock in silence – a sort of *grown-up* silence, if you know what I mean – and seeing how self-assured she was and the fact she was crisscrossing the world for her music career . . . it hadn't occurred to me she could be just a year or two out of high school.

I was so taken aback, I interrupted the conversation she was having. 'For real?' I asked.

It probably wasn't a smart thing to say. But Kita smiled and nodded.

I wasn't thrown for long. I figured there are some nineteen-year-olds who seldom leave their parents' house and spend their days sending gossipy texts, while others like Kita grow up fast into worldly souls.

The two of us had talked about heading over to Cronulla after dinner to see Matt Corby perform, but things were going so smoothly in the group that we stayed put. Ty and Lil were in good spirits and talking with Kita's friends.

When it was getting late, someone suggested we should all migrate up to this nightclub in the Junction, El Topo Basement. Next thing I knew, we were all piling into taxis. A quarter of an hour later, we filed into the club.

The thing is, I'm not the biggest fan of nightclubs, all the noise and booze and peacocking. I was relieved when a mate called, so I could step outside and talk to him and hear myself think. Kita told me later she thought I'd bailed on her. She'd said to herself, *Oh no, that didn't end well.*

I went back in and found her. For the first time since we'd met that morning, she looked uncomfortable. Maybe this wasn't her scene either.

'It's kind of a bit much,' I said.

'Yeah, it's a bit much. Let's go.'

So, we both smoke-bombed. All up, we were at the club for probably only forty-five minutes.

We kissed at the end of the night. And we talked about catching up soon, doing something fun in Los Angeles, my new flame's next port of call.

After leaving Kita, I was so euphoric and distracted that I left my phone in the back of a taxi. I thought it was gone for good. But this group of girls found it and texted me, and I retrieved it the next day.

My luck was in.

26

I WASTED NO TIME hauling myself to the States. I could justify it because my physiotherapist, Mark Kozuki, worked out of Newport, near enough to LA. I also had several mates living roundabouts, including Corey Wilson, a brilliant surf photographer. I figured I'd head directly from the US mainland to Hawaii for Pipe.

Even to myself, I didn't want to admit that I was gaga – Kita and I had had one date, for crying out loud. But there was no denying the urge to be around this girl.

In LA, we had a few more dates. I remember eating a lot of sushi, which Kita has a thing for. Just like in Australia, the time we shared was smooth and gave me that great-to-be-alive feeling, both during and afterwards. We chatted, we laughed and any quiet periods passed comfortably, as though our pairing had sprouted wings and didn't need hot air to keep it airborne.

One time, Kita came to Newport where I was staying at Corey's house. The waves were terrible, and we spent more time playing basketball than surfing. She was good, too. She could really play. She could also trash-talk: 'Hey stalker, you followed me to Australia and now you've followed me to America to get your ass whipped.'

Probably because we'd done that bushwalk on our first date, the idea of venturing into nature was a recurring theme with us. After learning Kita was infatuated with Yosemite National Park, I booked a place to stay with a sauna and hot tub that was fifteen minutes outside the park, thinking we'd go with Corey and this girl he liked. At the eleventh hour, however, Corey pulled out.

'Oh man, you've stitched me up,' I said, forcing a chuckle. 'Feels like a big step, don't you think? Going away already, just the two of us, hanging out 24/7 for three days and nights?'

Corey sympathised but said his hands were tied.

I couldn't do this to Kita without checking with her first.

'It's just us now,' I said. 'What do you want to do?'

'No, no, I'm keen,' she said. 'Let's go. Us two.'

I thought, *This girl is something else*. Nothing seemed to throw her.

'Hey Corey,' I said later. 'She wants to go with just me.'

He laughed. 'Maybe it's love, man.'

OUR WOOD CABIN WAS idyllic – simple, clean and cosy. The weather had turned chilly.

On our first day, we hit up the local Whole Foods Market. Because we were both into eating well, we spent a fair bit of time making our considered choices about what to stock up on. There was a lot of label-reading going on, as well as discussion about the meals we were going to prepare. It probably doesn't sound like a barrel of laughs, but because we were of the same mind, and because this was Kita, I was walking on air.

As a cook, I'm a bit of an improviser. I tend to throw a whole bunch of random ingredients into a pan, stir them up and voila! I'm usually content with the result but, looking back, maybe a lot of what I've whomped up in my time would have tasted like crap to anyone who knew their way around a kitchen.

On our second night at the stovetop, Kita was watching me.

'Hmmm, what are you making there exactly?'

'Speciality of the house.'

The night before, we'd eaten Mexican. On this night, I'd cooked pasta and was Mexicanising it with last night's leftovers. I can remember it tasting pretty good, but maybe I was still battered from Depot Bombie.

At Yosemite, Kita and I started talking at a deeper level than we'd done thus far. I told her about my upbringing – a lot of the stuff I've been telling you. While acknowledging the hard parts, Kita loved the sound of a bustling household, the energy generated when a family reaches critical mass. But there was an unspeakably sad backstory to her reaction. Two and a half years earlier, Kita's older sister and only sibling, Natassja (Tash), had died of lymphoma.

The Kita I got to know in Yosemite was a coloured-in version of the one I'd recognised at first glance: confident, mature (not just for her age; more mature than me) and free-spirited. She was also hyper-creative, forever writing or tinkering with lyrics, jotting down ideas the instant they came to her. Meanwhile, I might be in the same room journaling or meditating. I wasn't shy about doing those things in front or her. I could be myself.

Kita told me where, for her, the inspiration for writing songs came from. 'I need to be in a state of turmoil to write music that resonates with other people. The exception is being in nature and feeling calm, almost bored.'

'Turmoil, though – that works best?'

'Yep – heartache, pain. The writing is a therapy session for me because I put words to emotions that I wouldn't normally think about. I can piece together how I'm feeling.'

Sitting there on the page, she said, her lyrics could scream torment so vividly that people reading them might say, 'Oh my gosh, are you all right?' To which Kita would say, 'It's okay, step back. Let's just leave it as a song, shall we?'

At Yosemite, she'd keep a notepad and recorder handy. We'd be driving along, say, when suddenly she'd turn the music down, pull her recorder out of her bag and start humming a melody, which she'd revisit the next time she was in a studio.

It turned out she'd started watching surfing semi-regularly only after Mick's run-in with the great white. I liked that she had her own thing – her music – so there'd be lots to talk about there, and that she was curious about my thing and knew bits and pieces about it, but not the whole scene. She'd heard of a few people, but not a lot of detail.

Born in Brisbane, Kita had grown up in Port Macquarie on the Mid North Coast of New South Wales, nearly 600 kilometres from Culburra. Both Tash and Kita were musical from the get-go. Tash, who was five years older, could sing but really shone on guitar, while Kita sang like an angel. When Kita was in her mid-teens and Tash was home during university holidays, they'd perform at open-mic nights at a local bar called The Pier. It was while doing one of those that Kita was talent-spotted.

DURING OUR STAY, I received a call on my mobile while we were sitting under a waterfall. How the call reached me, I'll never know, because reception in the park was woeful.

The caller was my cousin Brooke, who's also one of my best mates. Choked up, she told me that her dad – my uncle Mark, Mum's brother – had died. He'd been for a surf, come home and had a heart attack.

Kita was watching me as I listened. Our eyes met, and it was clear she could tell something bad had happened. Not just bad, irreversible.

Uncle Mark was a legend of a bloke. A builder, he'd often have you crying with laughter with his stories and take on things. Brooke, one of his three daughters, was only a couple of months older than me. We were close growing up and stayed that way. Whenever I do anything with mates on the South Coast, I always invite Brooke.

I got off the phone and filled in Kita.

'You've got to go,' she said. 'You've got to go right now.'

My mind went into overdrive. I was thinking, *Hang on, I've got Pipe to go to. There's a world title on the line.* But Kita didn't see those things. She saw only loss and a clear path.

Within an hour, I'd decided I'd go home for the funeral, but didn't need to leave straight away. Kita and I could finish our trip. While the news of my uncle's death rocked me, it also triggered deeply painful memories for Kita. This shared suffering acted as an accelerant for our connection, taking our conversation into terrain we mightn't otherwise have ventured into for months. Amid the peace and majesty of Yosemite, Kita – and Kita alone – was there for me when I needed a compassionate ear. And I, in turn, was there for her.

For Kita, the news of my uncle's death released a fresh round of grief for her sister. Because she was just seventeen when Tash died, Kita did not yet possess any useful techniques for dealing with something so traumatic. Consequently, she'd tried to block it out and bury it, which never works.

In the past two years, Kita had made numerous attempts to let everything out in a perfectly worded song. Not for want of effort, however, she believed nothing she wrote did her sister or her own emotions justice. But the events of Yosemite brought a breakthrough. It was there that she conceived of 'Hotel', her cathartic song-for-Tash that would go double platinum.

On our last day in Yosemite, we sat on a mountaintop in the still coolness of dusk. Kita told me how her nan, her maternal grandmother, had been such a kind and constant presence throughout her childhood. Kita's parents had split up when she was two, forcing her mother to return to work as a dentist and her nan to step in as a caregiver. Towards the end of some days, Kita would become upset, missing her mum. Her nan would say, 'Don't worry, sweetie, your mummy will be home on the pink clouds.'

As Kita told me that story, the clouds over Yosemite turned pink before our eyes.

27

THE FUNERAL FOR MY uncle was held in Currarong, which was home to Brooke as well as Keegan and Ty. Following the service, we had a few nights out and I guess I couldn't stop raving about Kita.

'Do you love her?' Keegan asked.

'You know, I'm feeling that way, yeah,' I said.

'I have an inkling she's the one,' Keegan said. 'I think you're hooked.'

The funny thing was, I'd had the same sense when Keegan started seeing his girl, Rebecca. I remember thinking, *I should make the effort to befriend this girl, because she's going to be around for a while.* And she has been. They tied the knot in 2018.

After a week at home, it was time to return to the States. That's where all my gear was, where physio Mark was and where Kita was.

It was now mid-November 2015. Physically, I was feeling okay but not tip-top. I still had symptoms from Depot Bombie – though I didn't realise they had anything to do with Depot Bombie – which meant I was barely surfing. I was a surfer who was barely surfing because I couldn't: I didn't have the energy.

I still figured I'd be fit for Pipe, though. For a comp like Pipe, with so much at stake, I'd switch to emergency power.

I was still in contention for the world title, clustered with Medina and Mick, among others. If I could win Pipe and these other guys bombed, I could be world champion. It was a long shot but then again, after Fiji just about anything felt possible. I'd be underdone, I knew, but the thing about Pipe is, you can't cram for those waves. To have any hope of succeeding there, you need to have racked up hours and hours of practice over a period of years – and I had. With Mark's help, I was focused on getting my body right so I could have a red-hot go. Little did I know, my body wasn't the problem.

Meanwhile, Kita was preparing to enjoy one of the perks of her profession. Her management at the time, Tap Music, owned this mansion in the Hollywood Hills where they encouraged their signed artists to reside for short periods and get creative.

'Come up and stay with me,' Kita said.

'Sure.'

We spent about two weeks there, just the two of us, living like A-listers in a six-bedroom palace. We'd do something most mornings – go out for a bite, say – but come the afternoons, Kita would knuckle down to work and would often be up writing until 2 am. That seems to be how it works with musicians. They're a bunch of night owls – the opposite to surfers.

Kita and I had started talking about how we might work as a couple. We knew spending time together would be challenging because we'd both be flying all over the place, but I also believed that we'd find a way, that this – the two us – would be great.

'I'll finish my events then see where you are on the planet, and I'll head there,' I said. 'I mean, there's surf everywhere.

I'm free. I can go wherever I want, really. My fitness regime is portable. My life is mobile.'

The day arrived when I needed to leave for Hawaii. It was mid-morning. Shortly, a hire car would be purring out the front bound for LAX.

In the shower, I talked to myself, psyched myself up. *Just do it, man. Do it.*

Dressed and ready to go, I stuck my head into our room, where Kita was still asleep. I sat on the bed, waking her up.

'I don't want to see anyone else,' I said. 'Would you like to be my girlfriend?'

Kita smiled. 'Mark me down,' she said. 'It's just so nice that somebody would say that, and not just lead me on for ages.'

There were strong feelings on both sides, so what we did that morning was close the loop. We ended the uncertainty and she appreciated that.

Poor Kita. She had no idea what she was getting herself into.

28

HAD I LET MYSELF, I could have wallowed in the joy of my burgeoning relationship. But for the next few weeks, I resolved, I would become a surfer again. I'd make it my mission to conquer Pipe, to produce my best there. And if I did? Well, perhaps I'd return to Kita's embrace as the world champ.

I practised only at Pipe, notching one monster session after another. As the days passed, I couldn't have fallen off a wave if I'd tried. That's how it felt. Among the other surfers, I was hearing talk – buzz – about the waves I was catching and smashing, and how much of a threat I was going to be.

Sometimes, I'd stay out in the surf for two or three hours then return to the Rip Curl House and flake out. I was still battling waves of fatigue against which resistance was futile. I chatted with Kita most days, every day probably.

When Tyler finished competing in Maui, a few days before the start of Pipe, I asked her to visit me. One afternoon, we took a walk on the beach before sitting down on the sand. Tyler was tossing up whether to stick around and watch me compete, or head home to start her end-of-year break. She'd just finished fifth overall.

'I think you should stay,' I told her. I had this sense that something was going to happen but didn't know what it was. 'I think you need to be here.'

'Okay,' Tyler said. 'I'll stay.'

She threw a mattress on the floor and bunked down in my room. After all those years on the road with Dad, neither of us ever thought twice about sleeping that way.

All right. Now I'm going to tell you about that day: 10 December 2015. Thinking about it again, extracting the details from my mind's darkest vault, I get chills.

It was early morning. The competition would start within hours. I paddled out in the biggest waves I'd seen at Pipe. So thick. I paddled past everyone to the deepest point, deep inside and got this cracking wave straight off the bat. I rode the barrel – it was a rare thing to get a barrel that morning because the surf was so huge. I got spat out in the channel, where I lay on my board and started paddling back out.

Two guys were in the water near me. There was Mick. And there was New Zealander Ricardo Christie, a good guy.

My confidence was stratospheric to the point of tipping into nonchalance. It wasn't that I'd stopped respecting Pipe, more that it was comp time, and I was still surfing the place like Gerry Lopez, or so it felt.

On the way back out, this colossal set came in. As the first wave threatened to break right in front of me, I had nowhere to go. Everyone else was bailing their boards – swimming for the depths to get as far away from the impact as possible. Of course, when you do this, you get tea-bagged: your board stays on the surface and cops it, with the force of the wave running down your leg rope and all but yanking your leg out of its socket. But that's preferable to a direct hit.

The alternative to bailing is duck-diving while staying on

your board, in which case you'll get no more than half a metre underwater. That was the dumb option I chose – perhaps out of complacency, a momentary delusion of invincibility. My punishment was to have this fifteen-foot, second-reef Pipe wave land on top of me.

How do I describe the impact? I'm struggling to. I've never had a building collapse on me, and I realise that would kill you stone-dead. Yet it's hard for me to imagine how the building could feel weightier than this wave did. It knocked me sense-less. Apparently, when I surfaced, I was conscious but white as a sheet. Expressionless. A ghost.

I was still in the impact zone. What had hit me was only the first wave of a ten-wave set. One after another, arriving about twenty seconds apart, these watery avalanches came crashing down on top of me. Not thinking straight, I stayed on my board throughout the onslaught.

Finally, I made it to the beach. Ricardo was next to me. He'd been washed in.

I shuffled to the Rip Curl House, the whole way mutter-ing, 'Oh, I'm fucked, I'm fucked.'

Tyler was there. 'I got flogged,' I told her.

I tried eating some breakfast. But I could scarcely taste it. *What the fuck!* My sense of taste was gone.

I went to my room and lay down on my bed. I called Kita. Over and over, I told her the same thing I told Tyler: 'I got flogged.'

And then I fell asleep.

PART 3

REMEMBER, I'M IN YOUR CORNER

29

WHEN I CAME TO, I could hardly move. I tried calling out, but my words were slurred. Nick Pollet appeared at the doorway. He took one look at me and phoned for help from the paramedics who were on location.

Two promptly showed up. By then, more people had filed into my room – Tyler, Mick, Corey, Wilko. They were telling the paramedics that I'd said I'd been hammered in the surf. I was shaking uncontrollably, and I heard Mick say, 'Hold on.'

The paramedics carried me out of the house on a stretcher towards an ambulance. As they did, I looked into the eyes of my friends and sister and saw fear. I started to convulse. Then, I've been told, my eyes rolled back in my head and I passed out.

I woke up in the emergency room of a small hospital. Alongside Tyler was Mikey, who'd been free-surfing close by on the North Shore. Tyler had called him.

'We've stabilised you,' the doctor said, 'but we need to get you scanned. Try to relax.'

A short time later, I was wheeled off for CT scanning, then wheeled back to emergency.

Another half hour passed. Then two doctors appeared at my bedside.

'Your scans tell us that you have bleeding on the brain,' one of them said. 'There's also swelling.'

Both doctors were looking at me strangely, as though I were a puzzling case or something.

'It's best you be moved immediately to a larger hospital,' the other said.

So, I took another ambulance ride to this larger hospital.

I wasn't saying a great deal at this stage and what I was saying was hard to understand apparently, but Tyler discerned that I was asking for Kita. She got hold of my phone, found Kita's number and dialled it.

After filling in Kita on the morning's events, Tyler said, 'He really wants you over here. Can you come?'

Kita was in Australia, touring. She'd done a series of gigs in Sydney and had just wrapped her last show in Melbourne. When Tyler called, she was feeling a little worse for wear. She was also scheduled to spend another week in Melbourne in the studio, alongside Julia Stone among others, but dropped everything to come to me. Worried, tired and hung over, she left her favourite leather jacket at Tullamarine Airport.

Her manager queried her decision to go, but Kita was adamant. I found all this out later, of course. I found out a lot of what I'm telling you long after the event. Kita said she knew only this: *Owen needs me, and I've got to go.* She wasn't torn. My being hurt brought up Tash-related issues for her again. Since Tash's death, Kita had at times tormented herself with the thought that she hadn't been there enough for her sister. Even if that were true – and I'm not saying it is – she wasn't about to make the same mistake with me.

Along with Kita, my family flocked to my bedside. Joining Tyler and Mikey were Mum, Kirby and Kirby's husband Damien. I greeted each new arrival, not with a warm expression of gratitude but a surly insistence that I was fine.

'There's nothing wrong with me,' I'd say. 'Why are you here?'

There was no sign of my father, though. My father stayed home.

IN MY HOSPITAL BED, if I wasn't blurry or morose, I was aggressive. 'Get me the fuck out of here,' I'd snarl to anyone in earshot.

After two days, I could move though not well. I'd get out of bed, take a couple of shuffling steps and say, 'You see? I'm fucking fine.' But these were stupendously unimpressive displays of mobility. I was delusional; it took me several days to let go of the idea that I would return to Pipe and surf for the title.

The doctors didn't want to discharge me. I was in a precarious state, they said. Bleeding and swelling on the brain – these weren't conditions to be taken lightly, they said. In line with there being observable, physical damage to the brain, what I'd suffered went beyond concussion; it qualified as a traumatic brain injury (TBI). The difference between a concussion and a TBI, the doctors explained, lies in its severity and the presence of certain additional symptoms, such as slurred speech, confusion and convulsions, all of which I'd displayed. They put me on a bunch of medications, including anticoagulants and anticonvulsants.

Numerous times, I watched a doctor take some combination of Mum, Tyler and Kita aside and, with a grave expression, counsel them on the best course of action. This always involved me staying put for now.

One time, a doctor – I think he was a neurologist – came to my room while Kita was with me. For the hundredth time, I protested that I wanted to leave and return to Australia.

'You shouldn't be flying,' the doctor said.

'If I can't fly home,' I said, 'what would you have me do?'

'Well, you could be transferred to a rehabilitation facility specialising in brain injuries where you'd receive the appropriate care.'

'What is this?' asked Kita. 'You mean like a lunatic asylum?'

'No,' the doctor said, 'not a psychiatric hospital, a rehabilitation facility where your treatment *may* include a psychiatric component . . .'

Mum and Kirby were inclined to heed the doctors' advice, but in Kita, Tyler and me they faced a wall of resistance.

'He wants to get out of here,' Tyler said. 'What are we going to do – lock him up?'

The doctors held firm. 'Even if you leave the hospital, you might have to stay in Hawaii for a period of several months,' one said. 'We wouldn't want you to fly for, say, three months, because of the swelling.'

'Oh, fuck that,' I snapped. 'I'm getting out of here.'

The doctor ignored me. 'For a traumatic brain injury such as yours, you're looking at five to ten years for a full recovery.'

Five to ten years? Come off it, I thought. *I'm fine already.*

But this doctor was only warming up.

'Your brain looks like a blast victim's,' he said. 'You don't just have bleeding. You have multiple points of scarring – scarring and brain changes in four or five different areas. I'd compare the damage to the kind we see in blast victims from warzones or infants with shaken baby syndrome.'

Here we were in the surfing capital of the world, the doctor said, and yet I was the first surfer he knew of whose brain had been scanned and analysed. As he saw it, there were at least two intriguing possibilities: the kind of damage to the brain I'd suffered (not so much the bleeding and swelling, but the scarring) was exceedingly rare in surfers, or alternatively, it wasn't rare at all but going undetected.

'To be frank,' he said, 'it's hard to know exactly how this is going to play out for you. We'd be very interested to hear how you're getting on five to ten years from now. Please let us know.'

30

A LITTLE MORE THAN a week after I was admitted, the doctors started softening their attitude to me leaving. That wasn't because I was nailing the neurological tests they were giving me; I was flunking them. But I think the doctors figured I had the might of the WSL and Rip Curl behind me, as well as a loving family, and consequently I'd be looked after.

Mum wanted me to stay where I was. It's said that no one knows you better than your mother – they know when you're sick, sad or troubled. In her bones, Mum knew that I was crook and leaving hospital would be a mistake. But she was overruled, chiefly by me.

My family and Kita returned me to the Rip Curl House. But I was a wreck. I couldn't walk. I couldn't sit outside in the sun for more than three or four minutes before I'd start shaking uncontrollably, at which point two of the resident surfers would pick me up and carry me back to bed.

Both Mum and Kita moved in. Kita put her life on hold to care for me, which included washing me. Here's how it worked: two guys would carry me into the shower recess and plonk me on a stool beneath the stream of water.

'We'd better make you look good for Kita,' one of them would say, and he'd start playfully scrubbing under my armpits.

Then Kita would come in and wash me with a soapy flannel. She'd also shampoo my hair.

I was having difficulties on my left side. To my left, everything was blurry. Kita insisted that whenever I had visitors to my room, they should sit to my right – on the floor, never on the bed. The lights would be off and everyone had to speak very softly, almost at a whisper. Any stimulation coming from my left would cause me to shut down. I'd have to hold my head in both hands, close my eyes and tell everyone to be quiet. The latest injury was on the left side of my brain.

Some visitors walked out, shaking their heads: *Why's this guy out of hospital?*

One evening, there was a stunning sunset and a few of the guys shifted my bed to give me a perfect view. Kita lay down next to me and we watched the sky dim and stars appear. It was then I realised how lucky I was to have her with me. I turned my head to look at her, marvelling at her kindness and strength and beauty. Somehow, she could experience this ordeal moment to moment. She didn't appear to be thinking or worrying about when and how it would end. Because I wasn't of sound mind, I thought I was fine. But it would have been understandable if Kita had been wondering if I ever would be.

'I love you,' I said.

'I love you.'

SO MUCH OF THIS period is impossibly vague – but I can recall this next event distinctly.

I was sitting up in bed one afternoon, just after having something to eat. Mum, Tyler and Kita were all with me. Suddenly, every iota of strength left my body. I felt myself slump. While still conscious, in a sense, I was no longer in the Rip Curl House or Hawaii or anywhere else in this world. Instead, I'd gone to a different reality where I was floating amid bright colours.

There were two other beings with me, neither of whom I recognised. They weren't even human, more concentrations of light. They told me everything was all right, that I was going to be okay.

Then, as quickly as I'd left, I was back in bed in the Rip Curl House. I could hear Kita sobbing. She'd been present when Tash died, she told me later, and there was something about how I'd faded out that was frighteningly familiar.

What happened in those moments when I faded out? I don't know. Did I almost die? Was I crossing to the other side, whatever that is? I can't answer these questions with any certainty. But nor can I discount the possibility that the answer to both is 'yes'.

Much later, I read up on near-death experiences (NDEs). The conflict in science over NDEs centres not on whether they happen, but on what they are. Something like one in five people who are resuscitated after cardiac arrest report having had an NDE. No one resuscitated me – I came back of my own accord – but that's not the point here.

As strange as my experience was, it didn't contain all the elements of a classic NDE. I experienced bright light, a sense of being beyond what we think of as reality, and received reassuring words from what appeared to be supernatural beings – all typical elements of an NDE. But other common features were missing from my experience, including: seeing a tunnel that the experiencer perceives as a bridge between the life we know and an afterlife; visions of deceased relatives, who may guide the experiencer through a life review in which they feel again every emotion the past events aroused; and a sense of euphoria.

There was something else about my experience that was typical, which was a sense afterwards that what I'd experienced was real, even hyper-real. There was nothing hazy or dreamlike about it. It happened, pure and simple.

When trying to account for NDEs, researchers fall into one of two camps. The first argues that an NDE is a purely physiological phenomenon that occurs within an oxygen-starved brain. There's nothing mysterious about them, this camp argues. The second camp, however, contends that no theory based purely on the workings of the brain can account for all the characteristics of an NDE, and we should consider the possibility that consciousness can exist independent of a functioning brain, or at least that consciousness is more complex than we think.

Anyway, as I told you, whatever happened to me exactly, my sudden unresponsiveness spooked Kita. It disturbed Mum and Tyler, too, and shortly after coming around I was having another ride in an ambulance.

Back in hospital, staff hooked me up to a lot of machinery, trying to figure out what happened to me at the house. They never did.

Within an hour of being readmitted, I started singing from the same-old song sheet: *Get me the fuck out of here!* The tireless trio of Mum, Tyler and Kita stayed glued to me, and the reward for their devotion was hearing this same preposterous demand on loop.

A doctor would come in. 'How are we today?'

'Great,' I'd say.

One day, Jules swung by.

'How you doin', mate?'

'I'm fucking great.'

'Yeah, well, you're talking.'

'I'm walking, too.'

I got up and took a hesitant step or two, and it was obvious to Jules that I was so far from great it was laughable. I was much closer to rooted.

The doctors repeated their recommendation that I forget about leaving Hawaii; instead, I should spend a minimum of three months as an inpatient in a facility specialising in brain-injury recovery. There, they said, I could rest up while receiving daily physical and psychological treatment. Speech therapy would be available, too. Such a place, they said, offered me my best chance of completely recovering my previous level of functioning in the shortest possible time.

While it isn't strictly necessary for all or even most patients with my level of impairment to live fulltime in a rehab centre, the problem in my case was the ten-hour return flight to Australia. Plane travel was problematic in my condition, they said. They could all but guarantee an unpleasant experience, because high altitude increased cerebral blood flow and intracranial pressure. That said, they conceded, given that it was now two and a half weeks since my accident at Pipe and my symptoms were less severe than when I'd presented, the risk of any catastrophic outcome was slight.

That was all I needed to hear. I was determined to leave. Kita and Tyler backed me, Mum less so.

'Okay, we're going to do this,' Tyler said. 'We're going to get him home.'

31

COINCIDING WITH MY CRISIS, suffering spread through the Rip Curl House like measles. Mick received word from home that his brother Peter had died suddenly at the age of forty-three. Meanwhile, Bede broke and displaced his pelvis in a cover-your-eyes wipeout.

Ten interminable days and nights after my second admission, I was discharged. The doctors reluctantly approved my plan to fly, but urged me to report promptly to hospital once back in Australia.

Tyler and Kita tried to persuade the WSL to pay for a private jet to carry Bede and me home, but the WSL shared the doctors' nervousness and were unwilling to facilitate a flight. If I insisted on making my own arrangements, they said, they wanted a nurse to accompany me on the plane.

'I don't need a nurse,' I protested. I was carrying on, as usual. I was hard work.

'All right, then,' Kita said. 'We'll wing this.'

Tyler booked the three of us onto a commercial flight. 'We'll get you through this,' she and Kita promised.

Kita pushed me in a wheelchair through the terminal and onto the plane. We were in business class, thank heavens. I was in a window seat with Kita next to me, while Tyler was in the row in front. To minimise sensory stimulation, I donned dark sunglasses and noise-cancelling headphones, and Kita politely asked the flight attendants to refrain from talking to me.

The flight was an experience I'd like to forget but never will. At times, it was though I could feel my brain expanding. As my heart pounded and my T-shirt became clingy with sweat, I battled to subdue a sense of impending doom. I was convinced I could hear blood-curdling screams coming from inside the cabin. Had Kita and Tyler not been with me, reassuring me, I might well have come unstuck at 30,000 feet. These days, when my mind wanders back to this episode and my imagination runs wild, I picture the flight attendants trying to restrain me. When they can't because I have the strength of the possessed, burly male passengers swarm around and pin me, otherwise – who knows? – I might lunge for the exit door and hurl myself into the clouds.

I know now that had I travelled with a nurse, they would have sedated me when I was threatening to flip out. As it was, Kita and Tyler were left to do their darnedest with soothing sounds and words; it also helped when Kita gently lifted the cans from my head and covered my ears with her hands.

Those two were astonishing in the way they worked as a team. I'd have been inspired had I not been crazed. Tyler, especially, was a paragon of poise and level-headedness. As fine a surfer as she is, she might have missed her calling, my sister. She could have been a stellar tactical-response officer or the like. None of us slept a wink the whole ten hours. When we touched down in Sydney, it was like waking from a nightmare.

It was decided that Tyler would take me down to Mum's place in Gerringong, set me up in the spare room and the family would spend Christmas together. It was only a few days before Christmas, you see. So, Kita took a break from me at that point – an extremely well-earned break – heading north to Port Macquarie to see her mum's side of the family.

On Christmas Day, I called her.

'My family's gone out and left me alone,' I said. I was feeling a bit sorry for myself as I wasn't able to leave the house at that point.

The next day, Boxing Day, Kita drove the 500-odd kilometres from Port Macquarie to Gerringong, where she stayed with me for a few weeks.

I'll do my best to tell you about those three weeks. I say 'do my best' because my memory of them is sketchy, but here's the gist.

It mightn't surprise you to learn that I didn't report to a hospital as I'd assured my Hawaiian doctors I would. I did, however, check in with the WSL and Rip Curl, and moves were afoot to align me with a neurologist who'd steer my recovery. I was also in touch with a local clinic which, among other things, dispatched a walking frame to Mum's place.

I spent most of those three weeks in bed, either sitting up or lying down. The blinds stayed closed to keep the room dim. I wasn't up to reading or watching television – not even close. So, I mostly whiled away the hours dozing, blanking out or meditating. I felt constantly fuzzy and listless. Following doctors' advice, I did colouring in as a way of stimulating the brain's pathways to heal. A few times each day, I'd get out of bed and take a few steps, gripping my walking frame like the frailest geezer in an aged-care home.

The saddest times were the brief visits from my lifelong South Coast mates. I couldn't talk properly. Try as I might to sound normal, my speech was slow and slurred, as though I were toothless. After staying for ten or fifteen minutes, my visitors would then file out, fighting back tears. The state I was in shocked them. They'd known I was unwell, but who was this wreck of a man who'd once ridden the world's most challenging waves?

Though discomposed, they kept coming back. It wouldn't have occurred to them to abandon me, and leave Kita and my mother to do everything. They'd often swing by, together or one at a time, and help me walk the length of the house or, on bad days, support me as I shuffled from one room to another. Later, when I was feeling stronger, Keegan would come by on Fridays. He'd help me into his car and drive us down to the beach so we could look out to sea, watch the surf and talk shit. We were always trying to make light of it all.

WHERE SHOULD I HAVE been, if not in the spare room of my mother's home? I don't know. Kita thought she could manage my recovery by keeping my space peaceful. We'd thought that was part of the cure. But it wasn't. It was only a means of stabilising me, of preventing meltdowns.

Among my biggest problems, I see now, was my attitude. As debilitated as I was, I was adamant that I was all right, that I'd be better soon and back on the tour. I was in fantasyland. In the absence of my own good judgement, I needed someone to grip me by the shoulders, fix me with a hard gaze and tell me in words of one syllable how I was really faring: *Man, you're fucked. You need professional help.* And then frogmarch me to the nearest rehab facility, check me in and say: *See you in a month, bucko.* Failing that, I should have had a part- or fulltime nurse at home, who could have eased the burden on my mother and Kita.

I'm not blaming anyone for failing to be that teller of hard truths, least of all Kita. My God, she was nineteen at the time. Motivated by freshly minted love, kindness and lingering grief, she did all she could – more than any fair-minded invalid could have hoped for – to look after me.

So, I was delusional and obstinate, while Kita and others were infinitely patient. Thus the first month of my recovery – from late December 2016 to late January 2017 – was harder than it needed to be on everyone.

I SHOULDN'T GIVE THE impression that nothing was happening in respect to specialist care. In the same week that I returned from Hawaii, Rip Curl put me in touch with Drew Slimmon, the head doctor at Geelong Football Club. Drew had a special interest in concussion, which the Australian Football League (AFL) had begun to share when a growing body of former players revealed they were struggling with chronic neurological issues stemming, they argued, from repeat concussions sustained in their playing days.

Drew told me that, in his practice, he saw between twenty and thirty concussions per week, with recovery periods of up to three months. He'd seen my scans from Hawaii and, based on those, he said he wasn't going to treat me.

'Why's that?'

'You're not within my speciality. Your injury is at another level of severity. I might see you in three or four years. So, I'm going to refer you to Paul McCrory.'

Associate Professor Paul McCrory, I learned, was a neurologist who was recognised as a world expert in concussion and TBI. Previously, he'd served fifteen years as Collingwood's team doctor and had worked in Formula 1 motor racing, professional boxing and rugby, among other sports in which head injury is an omnipresent risk. He was based now at the Florey Institute of Neuroscience and Mental Health in the Melbourne suburb of Parkville, while also practising out of a second-floor clinic in Box Hill. This is where I met him in January 2016, Tyler having chauffeured me from the South Coast. (In March 2022, when I was writing this book, the AFL announced it was launching an independent review into Paul's work and advice around concussion over many years. For legal reasons and because I have nothing useful to say about it, I'm going to steer clear of that matter. I'm only going to tell you about my experience with Paul from 2016 onwards.)

'Nice to meet you,' Paul said, as I shook hands with a heavyset, middle-aged bloke with a round, boyish face and ruddy complexion.

Like Drew, Paul had reviewed my case notes. Unlike Drew, he wasn't deterred by the extent of the damage.

'You're on the mild side of what I see,' he said.

'I am?'

'Yes.'

Broadly, there are three levels of TBI: mild, moderate and severe. As debilitating as my TBI was, it was classed as mild. Behind that classification was the fact I hadn't displayed any clinical-level confusion or loss of memory for weeks afterwards. Minus those two elements, I fell short of being given a 'moderate' diagnosis. But apparently, a 'mild' diagnosis can be misleadingly reassuring. A lifetime of problems can ensue from a mild TBI. As for severe TBIs, these most often result from motor vehicle accidents; typically, they are open head injuries where the skull has been crushed and the patient will never be the same again. It's the old story, isn't it? As tough as you're doing it, there's always someone doing it tougher.

There was no way of knowing for sure whether I'd entered the surf at Pipeline with lingering swelling on the brain from one or more of my previous concussions. It's possible that the bombardment at Pipe was enough on its own to have put me in the state I was in. It was equally possible that it had taken me over the edge, that I'd entered the surf that morning vulnerable and exposed – and the ocean had punished me for my ignorance.

Paul was sanguine, though. From that first consultation, he had a knack for lifting my spirits. Calmly and reassuringly, he told me I'd be well again – it would just take time, probably up to a year until I felt fully myself again. All going to plan, he could see me back on the tour in 2017. If I could put up with the symptoms, he said, I could avoid going down what he called 'the pharmaceutical route'. Doctors prescribe a low-dose antidepressant to some of their TBI patients to help with their pain and cognitive symptoms. I figured I'd manage without it.

'You'll get through this, Owen,' Paul said. 'We'll get you back to surfing.'

There was nothing he could do for me in the short term. If he subjected me to an extensive neurological test now, he said, I wouldn't finish it let alone pass it. My brain wouldn't be up to the task of concentrating for more than a minute or two. He booked me in for another in-person meeting a couple of months hence.

'In the meantime,' he said, 'manage the symptoms as best you can and look after yourself. Sleep well, and when you feel ready, start doing a little gentle exercise.'

BACK HOME, KITA STAYED with me until her work could wait no longer. She was required in London, to write and record.

'You go,' I told her. 'I'm good. I've got people around. You go and do your thing.'

Reluctantly, she took off for the other side of the world.

Kita spent two weeks overseas – a productive period in which she reckons she wrote some of her best stuff, including 'Against the Water', inspired by our falling in love and sticking together when Kita could have run for the hills.

Travelling gentleman, welcome in
. . . Remember I'm in your corner when it's you against
the water

While Kita was away, Tyler sent her a photo of me standing out the front of Mum's place with a surfboard tucked under my arm. But that image was misleading in terms of how I was doing. I was still light-years away from being able to stand up on a moving board.

When Kita and I spoke during that fortnight, at times I felt and sounded bereft.

'I've been left alone over the weekend,' I'd say. 'I don't think I've eaten today.'

Kita was used to having long spells abroad, but not this time.

'I have to go,' she told her colleagues.

Initially, her management had been excited about the imagery of the musician and the surfer, but the extent of Kita's devotion to her stricken new beau perplexed them.

'Are you sure you want to do this for someone you don't really know?'

'Yes. And I *do* know him.'

Her colleagues knew better than to stand in her way. Take away an artist's sense of freedom and you kill their creativity – or so I'm told. They also guessed that Kita would spend only a week or two in Australia before jetting back to London. But that wasn't how things panned out. Not at all.

BY EARLY FEBRUARY 2016, Kita was back at my side but there remained a conspicuous absentee from the list of people who'd visited me since Hawaii. My father. I still hadn't laid eyes on him. I couldn't understand it. I was busted up about it, too.

Finally, on the phone to him one afternoon from the ocean pool in Gerringong, I spoke my mind.

'Man, I was in hospital for weeks. I almost died. I'm still in bad shape. I'm struggling to move around the house. I can't leave the house by myself because I get disoriented. I don't understand why you haven't been down to see me.'

'Oh,' Dad said. 'I didn't know it was so bad.'

I believed him then and still do now. I would learn later that, by the start of 2016, he was in the early stages of his own health crisis, which I'll tell you about later.

Dad did pay me a short visit that February. By then, Kita and I had left Mum's place in Gerringong and moved into Tyler's house in neighbouring Gerroa. Tyler was off surfing, preparing for the year, so Kita and I had the place to ourselves except for when my father stayed with us for a few days. These were bumpy because I was such heart-sinking company. But at least he came – that meant a lot to me. He drove me around, took me out and about, but at that stage there wasn't much he could do for me. It would be a few months before he would come into his own as a father.

At the end of February, Kita was booked to do some recording in Melbourne. She suggested I accompany her for a change of scenery. She drove us down and we checked into a hotel just outside the CBD and close to the studio she'd be working in.

Things went awry quickly. Every day, Kita spent hours working while I sat around in our hotel room feeling morose. Madly restless one day, I had the bright idea of going for a swim at a nearby public pool.

Sometime later, I called Kita from the footpath of a busy road.

'I don't know where I am,' I said. 'And I think I just almost drowned in the pool.'

I'm embarrassed recalling this. Kita had to leave the studio early, track me down and take me back to the hotel. She'd returned from London thinking I wasn't receiving the care I needed, but now felt out of her depth herself. We abandoned our Melbourne stay and Kita drove us back to the South Coast in a quiet car.

THOUGH PAUL HAD PREACHED patience, I'm not a particularly patient guy. To expedite my recovery, I was prepared to try almost anything.

For instance, I received treatment from a local chiropractor, who talked a good game about optimising my central nervous system so my brain and body could communicate more effectively. At my first session, he asked me to hit the floor and crawl. Down I went – and I couldn't do it. I couldn't figure out how to coordinate my opposing arms and legs. At subsequent sessions, as I improved, he'd ask me questions while I was crawling – super-basic stuff like 'What's your name?' or 'Where were you born?' I'd be slow to answer, if I could answer at all. The requirement to access my memory while performing a motor skill seemed to be overloading my system. It was demoralising. It was also one of the few times I detected alarm in Kita's face: *Holy crap,* her expression said. *This is hectic.*

Sometimes, Kita would drive me to these sessions. Other times, I'd catch the train or drive myself, but there was always a risk when she wasn't with me that I'd become lost and need to call her: *I don't know where I am. I can't find the car.*

At home, especially in the kitchen, I was an accident waiting to happen. I was forever burning food, and dropping glasses and cutlery.

But there were also milestones during those early months of 2016. At last, I could spend time outside in the sunshine without losing it – getting anxious and frustrated and eventually teary. Since the accident, I'd had trouble, psychologically and physiologically, with having my head underwater. Slowly, however, I graduated from dunking it in an ocean pool to dunking it in the ocean. That became the centrepiece of my day: heading down to the beach, dunking my melon and returning. Meanwhile, Paul encouraged me to increase, very gradually, the number of steps I was taking each day: 'If you walked this far today, aim to walk a little further tomorrow.' At that stage, we weren't dealing in the thousands or even hundreds of steps, but in the tens.

IN THE EARLY AUTUMN of 2016, I returned to Paul's clinic for our second face-to-face consultation. I wanted to be fresh when I saw him, because I had to do this neurological exam so he could gauge how far I'd come. He'd be measuring my abilities in reading, language use, attention span, processing speed, reasoning, memory and problem-solving.

I was nervous before I started so I was kind of joking around with him.

'I wouldn't be good at this, anyway,' I said, 'because I barely went to school.'

Paul said not to worry and just give it a go. All he wanted to do was measure how well my brain was working now. It wouldn't be terrible if I flunked. I'd get better eventually. It was all a question of time.

The exam went much like we both expected it to, I think. I couldn't complete it. Mentally, I ran out of steam.

But Paul made sure I left the clinic feeling upbeat. He said he was confident that I'd return to pro surfing. He would try to have me ready for the start of the next tour – 2017 – which had been his goal from the outset. In other words, he was writing off the whole of 2016. I hadn't done this up to that point, but I was almost glad he did because it allowed me to release a lot of the pressure I was putting on myself to get well. It encouraged me to imagine myself returning to the tour fully fit, rather than with a question mark the size of a Nazaré monster hanging over me.

TYLER'S GERROA PLACE HAD a lot going for it, not least a dazzling view of the ocean from the bedroom, as well as water glimpses from virtually every other room. But context is everything. It got to the point where that view and those glimpses were tormenting me, hour after hour, day after day. Had I been healthy, had I been surfing, then wonderful – I'd have relished eyeing the briny deep all day. But for as long as I was this land-bound sad-sack, for whom surfing again sometimes felt like a pipedream, then please, give me a break.

'I can't look at it anymore,' I told Kita.

We needed new digs. In March 2016, I bought us a little bush retreat in Berry, a quaint village-style town about twenty minutes west of Gerroa. A month later, we moved in. It was perfect. We had no neighbours within cooee, no traffic noise, just a restorative stillness from sunup to lights out.

'I feel like you're doing better here,' Kita said to me one morning over breakfast.

'I think you're right.'

I had more energy. We were doing yoga together and taking short daily walks, and I was helping in the kitchen without setting fire to anything. I was also painting. I'm no Rembrandt, but that wasn't the point – the point was to stimulate and exercise my brain. What did I paint? Well, waves, mainly.

All this was happening under the direction of Paul, who stressed the recuperative powers of routine. Because the wheels had been falling off, I'd had to keep restarting. I was so fragile – so many things could derail me. I viewed every small setback as a regression, but Paul discouraged that way of thinking. He said my recovery would feel stalled or even derailed at times, but I should push on, gently and sensibly.

Through my association with Aaron, among other factors, I already had alternative leanings with regards to diet, exercise and health. I was forever raising therapeutic ideas with Paul. What's your take on acupuncture? What about fish-oil supplements? Should I sit in a hyperbaric oxygen chamber? (I did a lot of that at a health facility in Wollongong, despite initially being rattled by the confined space; claustrophobia was another new companion of mine.) Paul's answer was always the same. It might help, or it might not; try it if you like, but keep your focus on the basics: sleep, diet and exercise.

Here's something else he said more than once, though not in these exact words: *Owen, you're going to be screwed until your brain decides that you're not.*

PEOPLE ASK ME WHETHER I felt guilty or embarrassed while Kita was caring for me. After all, they imply, here was this lovely songstress – possibly on the cusp of musical stardom – who was suddenly, at nineteen, stuck playing nurse to a man she'd known for a matter of months.

My answer is, not really. Though that's only because I was too discombobulated to see things from her perspective.

When a person has an injury like mine, the family and loved ones suffer the most. They live every day with the trauma and distress of it all, while the brain-addled person ends up forgetting most of it. I'm sure there were many times that, emotionally, I was in a better state than Kita, whose reward for caring for an athlete who'd metamorphosed into a sometimes despondent, sometimes surly invalid could be getting shut out or snapped at for no good reason.

Kita will tell you that she never resented the sacrifices she made. Her love for me, she says, brought her back from London. Why else, she asks, would she have dropped anchor in a bunch of small towns on the New South Wales South Coast she hadn't even known existed? I'll tell you this much: it wasn't because I was a great catch. No one who knew the shape I was in could have accused Kita of being attached to this hotshot surfer for the wrong reasons. Despite my own fantasies of a speedy return to the tour, it looked for all the world like I was done. I was barely functioning; I couldn't walk far or jog – the walking frame in my room said it all. None of my friends or the guys who looked after my finances thought I'd amount to anything much again. They saw me living out my days in the hills of Berry.

ON WAKING ONE MORNING in late March, Kita told me she felt odd.

'How do you mean?'

'I'm not sure.'

She went out for a while. When she returned, we went together into the bathroom. A minute or so later, she handed me a plastic pregnancy tester. I didn't have the slightest idea how to read it.

'Look at this,' she said.

'What is it? What does it mean?'

'It means I'm pregnant.'

(If you're wondering, *How did he manage that in the state he was in*? I don't blame you. I guess there are some abilities that don't desert us.)

We laughed and hugged. Despite all the reasons to be concerned about the timing, we weren't worried – or, at least, I wasn't. I was thrilled, maybe a little nervous, but nothing else.

We delivered the news to family members in several calls. Most of them received it the same way, emphasising the joy of it while not knowing how to address the practical challenges we'd inevitably face, particularly if I didn't get better or got worse, or indeed if I *did* get better and was off surfing for weeks or months at a time . . . never mind the effect on Kita's career.

Worrying about all that could wait for another day – that was the collective attitude. The exception was my mother.

My mother was somewhat of an expert on parenting. She had raised five kids who were all into extreme sports. Her level of love and care was unparalleled in my life. She had been taking care of me the best she could despite how moody and forgetful I was at the time.

Upon delivering the news to her, my mother panicked and held both our hands. The look on her face said it all. I knew my mother was coming from a place of care, but it was still difficult for Kita and I to hear the words: *How will you manage?* I think it was the first time we'd had to face the realities of raising a child and my condition.

By this stage, Kita was reconciling herself to the idea that this suboptimal version of me was permanent. She wasn't going to waste energy hoping I'd revert; she accepted me as I was. For me, however, knowing a child was coming spurred me on; it was another reason to get better rapidly.

Though Kita had long wanted to be a touring musician, she wanted something else more: to be with a man she loved and who loved her, and to raise her children in a family that would never break apart. To create such a family, she reasoned, you couldn't have both parents constantly crisscrossing the world. If I returned to the tour one day, something would have to give, and if that was her music career, so be it.

'I won't be a part-time mother who depends on a fulltime nanny,' she said. 'I can't do that. They'll be my kids, and I'll raise them. And maybe one day, when you retire, I can think about reviving my career.'

IN APRIL, WE HIT a rough patch. Kita was dealing with morning sickness and the hormonal cascade of pregnancy, while I was preoccupied with my recovery. Communication between us was out the door.

'It's like we've put our brains in a blender – that's how unified our thinking is,' she said.

She had to get away. She told me she needed time and space, and pointed her car towards Port Macquarie. On the way, she called my brother Tim.

'I still love him, but I don't know how to do this anymore – be there for him and be pregnant,' she said.

'This isn't him, Kita – remember that,' Tim said. 'This isn't him.'

'Well, I *can't* remember that,' she said. 'Because this is our time together. This is it, mostly.'

Then something remarkable happened.

It was a weekday morning. I was in the oxygen chamber in Wollongong. Suddenly – and this is the only way I can think to describe it – my consciousness shifted from one part of my brain into another. I felt this great distance open up from what had happened at Pipeline to the present day. It was a case of: *Whoa, what just happened? How did I get here?*

This is going to be hard for you to grasp, but I felt simultaneously better and worse. While my mind felt clearer and I was more present in the moment, I was also thinking, *Oh my*

God! I've lost my memory. I've lost everything. What's going on? It was scary. In an instant, a block of my life – specifically, great slabs of the last few months – had been erased. I didn't even remember getting into the chamber.

At the same time, I now grasped something fundamental with absolute certainty: I had been badly injured at Pipeline. Since then, I had never been fine, okay, all right or great; I had been a mess.

I got out of the chamber and called Paul.

'Something's happened,' I said. 'I don't know what it is exactly but it's something.' I was fearing the worst. As best I could, I explained what I'd felt in the chamber.

'Owen, you've made a great leap forward,' Paul said.

It took some long, candid conversations with Kita and my family for me to realise that Paul was right. What had occurred in the chamber was progress. My family told me how hard I'd been to deal with; how I'd been forgetful, moody and irrational. Apparently, I'd ask the same question four or five times a day, such as: 'Where are my surfboards?' My misplaced positivity about the state of my health – all this nonsense about being good and ready to surf again, and in need of no one's help – had worn thin.

My brother-in-law Damo reminded me of a conversation we'd had. 'You think you can surf, yeah? You think you could do an air?'

'Yeah, I could easily do that,' I said. 'I just don't want to right now.'

'Okay, well maybe just spin around, see how that feels.'

I'd tried to spin around and apparently passed out for forty-five minutes.

The last three and a half months were blurry, but my memories of most things preceding Pipeline were sharper, as was my conception of the present. Paul nailed it when he said it probably felt like a ghost of me had been living my life since Pipeline. Now I'd exorcised the ghost and I, the Owen I'd been beforehand, was in control again. Out of the boot and back in the driver's seat.

Remember, though, my reawakening occurred while Kita was on the open road – pregnant, miserable, confused – sailing away from the tangled web our relationship had become.

She'd reached Sydney when I called her with the news: *I'm back, but I've forgotten plenty.*

Unsure how to interpret that, Kita pressed on. She made it as far as Newcastle, where she stopped to visit a friend to whom she unloaded her troubles.

'What do I do?' she asked.

'Turn around,' her friend told her. 'Turn around and go back to him.'

And that's what she did.

IN ANOTHER CHAT WITH Paul, I told him more about how strange things were.

'There are all these things that have happened,' I said. 'We're newly pregnant. We've bought a house. And I've lost those threads. Kita has had to catch me up.'

Typically, Paul was unperturbed. This latest development was common in patients like me, he said. For the last few months, my traumatised brain had been incapable of laying down memories by the normal mechanisms. Instead of entering into my brain's filing cabinet, so to speak, these recent experiences were floating in front of an open window, blowing in the breeze. They weren't gone forever, necessarily; they'd probably come back to me at some time.

He was right about that. I began waking in a sweat several times a night, after forgotten memories popped back into my head. Most of the time, I recognised them as genuine memories, but that's not to say they always made sense to me, or that I could file them in their correct time and place. These memories were pieces in a puzzle, scattered everywhere and awaiting assembly.

For the first time, I could see the situation from my family's perspective, in particular my mother's. I'd been with Kita only briefly before I was hurt, yet it was she and not my mother who had taken on the role of primary caregiver. I think Mum had felt sidelined by this newcomer.

I could also consider more clearly the issue of where I should have been in those first weeks and months after Hawaii. I asked people: *Why wasn't I in a clinic? Why wasn't I taken to this doctor? Why, why, why?* The answer I received was that no one knew what to do with this lump of a lad, who'd been running his own race since he was nineteen, and who was unremittingly adamant there was nothing wrong with him that a little rest wouldn't fix.

For Kita, this was an excruciating period. She was carrying our child, yet it felt to her as though we were dating all over again because, for me, so much of our shared experience had been wiped out – not all of it, but a lot of it (I remembered telling her I loved her in Hawaii; that was something). She found this hard to believe, or hard to accept. The only consolation was that I was better equipped than I'd been in months to support her.

And she needed support. Upon waking, one of the first things I realised was that my girlfriend was exhausted and distressed. I had at least two jobs now: to get better and save our relationship.

And that's when my dad came to the rescue.

32

IN THE WINTER OF 2016, my father visited me for the second time since Pipeline, staying with Kita and me for a month at our Berry hideaway. It turned out to be one of the most important months of my life.

Timing is everything. In the past, Dad's stolid demeanour and preachy tendencies could drive me nuts, but both were perfect for these circumstances. Physically, I was on the mend, if slowly. Mentally, I felt daunted by the changes and challenges life was hurling at Kita and me.

Head injuries are complicated. You improve, but things seem worse because you understand more. You make connections and join dots then realise what a mess your life has become. That's why people with head injuries get so lost; they're convinced that they're sliding even as they're getting better. I needed setting straight.

Dad and I spent many hours on the deck, taking in the towering jagged cliffs jutting from a creek-lined ravine. Mostly, Dad talked and I listened, not detachedly or politely, but with focus, appreciation and, as the days and weeks passed, a growing sense of optimism and purpose.

'I'm so happy about what's happening in your life,' he began one late afternoon, as the sun slowly took its leave and the air turned a still and bracing cold. 'Becoming a father is going to be a special thing. Look, mate, in life you have one woman and that's it. Kita is a great girl. You've made your choice and that's where it sits. Once you accept that, once you let go of any what-ifs and could-have-beens – not just for a month or a year but forever – life becomes simpler. The path you need to follow stretches out before you. At this point, you're not technically a husband, but you may as well be. This past year, from everything you've told me, Kita has cared for you with as much patience and devotion as any man could hope for from his wife. She's young, she's far from home and she's sacrificed a lot for you. Now that she's carrying your child, you have responsibilities to her that go far beyond being a good man. Meeting that responsibility starts with creating a protective ring around Kita. If people are looking to breach that protective ring, well, you need to stand in front of her and make it clear that no one and nothing is going to break through. Once you've chosen a partner – and she's chosen you – you enter a different stage of your life. And when your first child is born, your life changes again and there's no turning back. At that point, you take on a duty, which is to raise strong, independent, clear-thinking children who know the difference between right and wrong, and you do that by setting an example. From the moment your first child is born, you'll find that your past life – all that happened before you became a father – ceases to matter. It'll be as though there was no life before that moment.'

Dad was as loquacious as I'd ever heard him, and I was lapping up his every word. In content and tone, he was giving me the opposite to what I'd been hearing and sensing of late from Mum and my sisters. This was essentially a big bowl of caution and doubt, served with the best of intentions though it was.

My father wasn't deluding himself about the fate of his own marriage. He knew it was over. But he maintained that my mother remained his one true love and he would never look at another woman. There was Mum and there were his five children, and that was all he'd ever need, he said.

Someone else loving my father's input was Kita. Though she wasn't directly involved in these father–son chats, she was roundabouts and heard more than enough to glean the cut-through purity and soundness of his message. She could see the transformative effect it was having on me, too: her broken man was being schooled in the ways of old-fashioned manhood; he was being urged to fight to reclaim his life and lay the foundations for a stable family. Just when Kita had been thinking about how impossibly dense the jungle of family dynamics could be, along came this straight-talking gent whose words were like the world's sharpest scythe.

Dad ran me through some exercises he used to do. Once upon a time, he did a lot of tai chi, so we did that together in Berry, slowing everything down, especially our breathing. It was the perfect prelude to us surfing together for the first time in years.

By this stage, I'd crept back into the ocean with a board, but my rhythm and coordination were missing. I was surfing like a beginner on a longboard, selecting puny waves and gingerly standing up before heading arrow-straight. That had been until a few weeks ago, when I'd stopped surfing altogether because

I was a basket case – I'd been unprepared to add relearning my craft to my to-do list. Now, galvanised by my father's words, the time felt right to venture back out. My father was smart enough to recognise that surfing was a part of who I was, and that I wouldn't truly be myself again until I'd reembraced it.

Just after six o'clock one July morning, we rose, took a walk, suited up, packed Dad's car and drove to the beach at Gerringong, about a half-hour trip on a lot of downhill, winding roads. We'd picked a morning when the surf was going to be on the small side. Nothing too intimidating, thank you.

'You know, I'm over the moon for you,' my father said as he drove. 'All these steps that I would want a son of mine to take, you're taking them.'

'Thanks.'

'Are you sure you're all right with this – surfing this morning?'

'I know I can surf. I can't feel the way I do right now and not surf.'

At Gerringong, we trotted down the beach to the shore, attached our leg ropes, waded out a little and started paddling out. The first wave we came to, I shut my eyes and duck-dived. Underwater, I felt a surge of panic. *Okay*, I thought, *let's keep the duck dives to a minimum.*

My surfing that morning was a long way from great, but it wasn't terrible either. Basically, I was a much slower, clumsier version of my fully operative self. But I could turn. I could surf.

One time I caught Dad's eye. He was beaming.

'You look exactly like you always did,' he called out. 'You're going great.'

He was pumped up. I hadn't seen him this happy since those surf trips to Indonesia.

On the ride home, he presented an intriguing idea to me.

'You know, why don't you and Kita come live with me at Lennox Head? I'll move some people out of the granny flat. It'll be like your own place. You'll be back on the coast, across the road from the beach. We can surf every morning, and I can drive you to the places you need to get to for your rehab.'

All I said at the time was something like, 'Hmm, interesting.' But he'd grabbed my attention. The way he'd couched the plan, it was all about me. But I could see plenty of upside for Kita, too. She was struggling on the South Coast. She was concerned about how my family might be perceiving her: this girl from Instagram who, virtually overnight, had become the central figure in my upturned life; this girl with whom I was now living in the scrub at Berry; this girl whose story I had recently in large part forgotten; this girl who was carrying my child. Kita had already floated the concept of shifting north, nearer to her roots, friends and spiritual home, and I was inclined towards doing anything I could to make her happy.

I spoke with Paul. While it was pleasing that I'd learned to relax more in the Berry shack, he said, there was a risk I was now becoming a little too relaxed, comfortable and complacent.

'You're going to have to leave there,' he said. 'You're going to have to be pushed again because you've stopped pushing. There's a chance that, if you stay there and spend your days on the couch, you won't ever get off it. You need to get back to the ocean.'

225

Kita and I thrashed out my father's proposition. A granny flat sounds small, I know, but this one was on the roomy side – two bedrooms (so, a dedicated nursery), one bathroom, and an open-plan kitchen and living area. My father would be close by in the main house but we'd have our privacy, our own space. Kita had friends in the area, and God knows she needed friends back in her life after an overdose of a high-maintenance me.

One complication was that Kita was at the end of her second trimester and had already chosen a midwife on the South Coast to deliver our child in a homebirth.

'We can move if we can find a midwife up there,' Kita said.

She hopped straight on the case and ended up calling the first midwife who popped up in a search – Bronwyn Moir from the Lismore Birth House. Bronwyn said that while her preference was to work with mothers and mothers-to-be from early in their pregnancy, she'd just had a cancellation and would make an exception for us. Kita thought Bronwyn sounded lovely.

So, in August 2016, about two weeks after my father had ended his stay with us in Berry, we packed up and moved north. The irony of it all didn't escape me. Eight years earlier, when Dad bought the house in Lennox Head and uprooted the family from Culburra, I'd fumed and sulked and refused to set foot on the property. Now, with my pregnant girlfriend and a loaded car, I was knocking on his door, not begrudgingly but with a sense of excitement.

It was a chance to begin anew.

PART 4

JUST STAY ON YOUR BOARD

33

IT WAS LIKE OLD times. Dad and I surfed in the early mornings, and ever so slowly my skills started to sharpen. It was a case of trying to remaster the basics – and I mean the absolute basics – then adding elements one by one. I couldn't fault Dad. He was patient, understanding and encouraging; it was as though he were blind to the losses and could see only the effort and progress. I still wasn't strong enough to surf every day – every other day was my limit.

As well as being my surfing partner and morale-booster, Dad largely relieved Kita of the role of taxi driver. He ferried me to my various TBI-related appointments, which were mostly on the Gold Coast or as far north as Brisbane. In the car, the chat was always upbeat.

'How are you feeling?' Dad asked one morning on the way to an acupuncture session.

'Yeah, pretty good. Getting there, I think.'

'You know what's happening now, right? You're reclaiming your life.'

'That's the way it feels, yeah.'

'You're going to be a champion again, you know?'

'Hmm, maybe. I hope so.'

'You will. Trust me.'

We drove on in silence for a while, then Dad piped up again.

'Is Kita okay? Is she happy here?'

'Yep. She has friends around. You're pitching in. She's good.'

'That's good. That's very good to hear.'

IN MID-OCTOBER 2016, Tim, Mikey, Kita and I gathered around the television at Mikey's place at Tweed Heads to watch the conclusion of the Roxy Pro France, where Tyler was poised to claim the world championship – a first for our family. Given our father's passion for surfing, which he passed on to us kids, you could say this day was more than fifty years in the making. Some of my earliest memories are of Dad talking about one or more of us winning a world title one day. The idea seeped into my brain, I can tell you.

Tyler had been the year's standout surfer from the outset, winning three of the first four events. In France, the world title was Tyler's the instant her nearest rival, Courtney Conlogue, lost in the semifinals. This unleashed unbridled celebrations in Mikey's lounge room. In the final against Carissa Moore, Tyler wore my No. 3 jersey instead of her usual No. 13. After she'd ridden her first wave, she pointed to the number. She lost the final, but it didn't matter. She dedicated her title win to Uncle Mark.

Tyler had excelled in the hardest year of my life. Coincidence? I don't think so. Don't get me wrong: this was Tyler's triumph. But I reckon she gained some personal growth and perspective from my ordeal. When I saw my father the next day, he was chuffed about Tyler's victory. Chuffed and proud.

IN NOVEMBER, MY RECOVERY hit a setback in the shape of various symptoms brought on by exercise. A simple walk would raise my heart rate to 120 beats per minute (bpm), up from a resting rate of less than 70; a fast-paced walk could see it skyrocket to 160 bpm. I was also bone-weary a lot of the time, too tired to surf and more inclined to lie down and nap at the oddest times. Kita voiced her concern that my capabilities had diminished, and I could only agree with her. I felt like I was going backwards at a time when Paul had predicted I'd be almost ready to resume my place on the tour. He'd said he hoped I'd be right in twelve months. Well, eleven months had elapsed and I was a shambles again. I was losing faith in the guy who'd been my oracle.

I wanted to be reassessed, in person, thus ruling out Paul. So I saw a doctor on the Gold Coast, a South African–born guy who was linked to Surfing Australia and knew a lot about concussion, having worked closely with football teams from multiple codes. I told him my story and he examined me. He advised that now might be the right time for me to introduce an antidepressant into my treatment plan. He gave me a prescription, which I put into a pocket of my shorts.

All along, Paul's position on meds had been that they were helpful for some TBI patients and very much an individual choice; the question to ask myself was whether I felt I could manage without them. I put aside my fading faith in Paul and turned to him for his thoughts on this latest turn of events.

'My advice would be to start from scratch again,' he said on a Skype video call. 'Walk around the oval. Just one lap. Do that for a week. Then up it to two laps. I want to remind you that it's completely normal at this stage for you to feel tired and even wiped out.'

'But why am I going backwards?'

Paul insisted that I wasn't; in fact, I was much better than I'd been a month or two ago, though it may not feel like it. What was happening, he said, was that my brain and body were communicating in ways they hadn't done since Pipeline. Up until now, he explained, when called on to exert itself, my body had relied on willpower to get moving. Now, the old mechanisms were grinding up again and there were gremlins in the system. But don't worry, he said, this would sort itself out over the next few weeks. 'Not a setback, Owen,' he said. 'This is exactly what is supposed to happen.'

From his desk, Paul picked up a pen and pad of paper. 'Let me show what recovery from a TBI typically looks like,' he said.

Paul drew two small circles, one at the bottom of the page and the other at the top. The bottom circle represented the starting point of my recovery with the top circle being the endpoint. He then drew a line from the bottom circle to the top one, but it wasn't a straight line – it looked like the old Zig Zag Railway. When it had almost reached the top circle, Paul gave it a sharp and extended downward spike, followed by a similarly steep upward spike that brought it into contact with the circle.

Okay, I thought. *I think I get it.* He was showing me that recovery from the kind of injury I'd suffered isn't linear, that

I should regard any apparent setback as inevitable and even welcome it, insofar as it represented another part of the process negotiated.

'So,' I said. 'Push on?'

'Yes. The medications might be useful down the track to handle side effects that crop up once you're back on tour, but for now you still have a lot of life to resume.'

'Back to square one, then?'

'Back to square one.'

I pared back the mileage of my morning walks before building it back up again, all the while monitoring my heart rate, which seemed to settle down. At this point, I resumed surfing for short periods. It was the same deal with surfing: get comfortable on two-foot waves, then four-foot, then six-foot. I went on a surfing trip with Mick to South Stradbroke Island, Queensland, and I tested myself in a QS event in Newcastle. Paul then talked to the WSL, reassuring them that I was ready to compete again. The WSL granted me an injury wildcard for the 2017 tour.

I'd be coming back.

KITA FAVOURED A HOME water birth for our baby. She said she wanted to feel as relaxed as possible during the labour and delivery, and that being in a clinical setting wouldn't create that feeling. She told her obstetrician her plan. We agreed that, come the time, if there were any complications, we'd beeline it to the nearest hospital. Midwives Bron and Bree visited us every other day leading up to the birth, making sure the baby was in the right position and that all was well with Kita.

About 9 pm on 1 December, as we were sitting around chatting in the lounge room of our granny flat, Kita started having contractions. She put one of her favourite distractions on the TV, *Keeping Up with the Kardashians*, while I called Bron.

'Okay,' Bron said, 'let us know when the pitch of Kita's voice starts to rise.'

By 10 pm, I was back on the phone. 'Things seem to be kicking in pretty solidly,' I said.

'Okay,' said Bron, 'we'll gather our things and come over.'

The hours passed. No sign of them.

'Where are they?' Kita said several times with increasing urgency, as though reading my mind.

Finally, at 1 am, they appeared at the door. I greeted them gratefully and they breezed in like they were about to see a movie. You could tell they'd been in this game for a while. It seemed they knew in which circumstances they needn't rush.

I got busy setting up the portable, blow-up birthing bath, which you fill with warm water mimicking the temperature inside the womb. Kita had spent some time in the shower, with me playing the role of human chair. By this time, I was tired and very low on energy. Bree was putting small chunks of bread into my mouth to keep me awake, although that was possibly unnecessary because Kita believed in vocal expression during the throes of labour and I'm not sure anyone in the same postcode would have been asleep.

We were in the bedroom when Kita noticed it was sunrise.

'Hell, we've been going all night,' she said. 'I'd better get this kid out now.'

She moved to the tub. She was probably in there for only half an hour before our son was born. I found myself laughing and crying at the same time. Kita was famished. I made her serve after serve of Vegemite on toast until she'd worked her way through an entire loaf of bread.

We'd chosen the name Vali months ago. If our child had been a girl, she still would have been called Vali. Kita had seen the name in the draft of a song written by her friend Lisa Mitchell and liked it, as did I. There's also a Vali, or Váli, in Norse mythology: he's a son of Odin and the giantess Rindr, and a brother of Thor. We gave our Vali the middle name Nalu, which means 'surging surf' in Hawaiian.

Of course, we were unprepared for the realities of day-to-day parenting. Our sleep was shot to bits, and we were unsure what to do half the time. But we blundered through, because what choice do you have?

Days after Vali was born, my mother broke it to me that she needed a second operation to remove a new tumour on her brain. The surgery had been booked some time ago, but she'd kept silent so Kita and I could focus on Vali's birth.

Two weeks after Vali's arrival, shortly before Christmas, Kita, Vali and I drove the ten hours south to Sydney to visit Mum in hospital before her operation. Kita and I had debated whether we should travel so far with a newborn, but in the end, Kita decided we had to.

'This is Vali's Ma we're talking about,' she said.

The trip was hard going. We had to stop frequently to settle Vali, who puked like a geyser just north of Forster. At the hospital, we found Mum in good spirits. The combined efforts of Tyler, Kelly Slater and Layne Beachley had helped to secure Charlie Teo to perform the operation, which went smoothly. Mum was going to be okay.

'YOU KNOW, YOU'RE GOING to win your first event back on tour,' my father said to me one morning.

It was the new year of 2017. The season opener, the Quiksilver Pro Gold Coast at Snapper Rocks, was due to start in mid-March.

'I don't know, man,' I said. 'I can't even surf properly.'

'You're going to do it,' Dad repeated.

'Oh, dude, you're off your head.'

'Just you wait. It'll happen.'

Dad didn't let up with his outlandish prediction. Every day, multiple times a day, it was: 'You're going to win your first event back.' It became like a mantra.

For Dad, it wasn't just empty talk. I could tell he meant it. And he backed up his words with practical help. He was still driving me all over the place for my treatments, and coming down to Boulders to sit with Kita and Vali while I surfed. I remember it as a precious time, ensconced in this small and loving three-generational family bookended by my high-principled father and my adorable son.

'This talk of me winning is probably crazy,' I said to Kita one night, shortly after we'd got Vali off to sleep. 'But, you know, if I'm going to come back, I might as well believe it.'

34

BY THE TIME SNAPPER came around, had I convinced myself that I could win? How should I put this? Absolutely, categorically no. Had it not been for my father's refrain, the idea of winning would not have occurred to me. The process of healing tended to fix me in the present. My waking hours were spent trying to get by, to function, to adhere to my routines. I wasn't in a headspace for projection, much less fantasy.

I had a new coach in my corner: Glenn Hall, known to everybody in surfing as 'Micro'. I'd been planning on partnering with Micro in 2016 – alas, that didn't work out – and he'd guided Tyler to her world title instead in what was his first year of fulltime coaching.

From Umina on the New South Wales Central Coast, Micro had spent his twenties trying to crack the tour through the QS. Success came at last when he was thirty-one, but in June of his rookie year, 2013, he fractured three vertebrae in his lower back at Restaurants – a reef break in Fiji – and vanished from the tour until 2015. He retired from pro surfing at the end of that year.

As a competitor, Micro had been a student of surfing, who'd break down the mechanics of the myriad manoeuvres and find improvement by finetuning his technique. This approach helped prepare him for the sideways move into coaching. He was more than just a technician and an astute strategist, though. A good talker and a better listener, Micro wanted to know his athletes as people and help them thrive out of the surf as well as in it. Anytime I was in his company, it was written on his face that he cared about me.

In the weeks preceding Snapper, I'd been party to several arguments among family about whether I should be competing at all. Only Dad was all for it; Kita had reservations but was prepared to back my judgement. Mum, Tyler and Mikey, however, all believed I was rushing things. What I'd say now is that, based on the evidence available at the time, theirs was a perfectly reasonable position.

For example, just a week out from the event, as part of a preseason training camp at Byron Bay, I took part in a soft-sand session at the Suffolk Park end of Tallow Beach under the former rugby league international Chris Heighington, who'd moved into sports performance after ending his 300-game NRL career. One drill entailed sprinting between a handful of cones. You were supposed to sprint to the first cone, bend down and touch it, then take off for the next one. Speed was the goal: touch all the cones in as short a time as possible. Don't hold back.

Chris said 'Go' and off I went. In my mind, I was flying. In my mind, I was as quick and agile as I'd ever been. I finished the course and looked at Chris and Micro. They seemed stoked for me. *Well done*, they were saying. *Great job.*

It was two or three years later that Micro, who'd filmed the session, finally showed me footage of that drill.

'Holy shit,' I said. '*Holy shit*. I was moving that bad?'

Micro nodded.

What I saw was a skinny guy lumbering between the cones, a skinny guy who wasn't even touching the cones like he was meant to. What he'd do was snail up to one, barely bend at the waist, and his hand would sail over the target. It was embarrassing and slightly horrifying. Thank goodness, Micro didn't show me the footage at the time. If he had, I think I'd have withdrawn from Snapper on the spot. I think I might have retired from surfing altogether.

By this stage, I'd progressed to surfing for up to one hour with what I'd call a relaxed intensity. That would have been okay if I were a free-surfer, but it was well short of where I needed to be on the eve of an event. I was biting my nails. The deadline pressure was causing me to *blow out all my circuits* – that's how I was describing the way I was feeling to myself. At night, I was too wired to sleep. By day, I felt wiped out.

I phoned Paul and told him I wasn't sure I was ready.

'Do a heat and we'll see how you pull up,' he said. 'Then we'll know a lot more.'

My sense was that Paul didn't expect me to go deep at Snapper. I think he thought I might be capable of winning a heat or two, at which point I'd withdraw from the event and from the next one at Bells, too.

My comeback was the subject of media interest from which the WSL sheltered me, making no requests of me to do interviews. For that, I was grateful. The last thing I needed was to be grilled on my darkest times, how I was feeling now and my hopes for the year. I would have been vague and evasive, and I don't like to be those things.

Normally, in the days before an event, I'd mostly be down at the beach, surfing a few times a day, training at the gym, tuning boards, and fulfilling media and sponsor commitments. But not this time. At Snapper, I was surfing once a day for half an hour. That was all I could manage. I was doing no other training, and there was no media, schmoozing, socialising or hanging out at the beach.

Instead, when I finished surfing, I'd rejoin Kita and Vali, and we'd chill in this palatial unit we were staying in. It belonged to Rip Curl's co-founder, Doug 'Claw' Warbrick, who offered it to me for the duration of the event. It was the penthouse in a block situated right in front of the wave. Kita and I didn't encourage anyone to visit let alone crash. The only active thing I did there was to take my skateboard down to the basement and ask my body to emulate some of the movements of surfing.

When the day arrived, Micro could tell I was having doubts.

'It's just thirty minutes, mate,' he said. 'Just stay on your board for two waves. Take off next to the rocks, stay on your board for two waves and see what happens. As for what you do on the wave, just let it happen.'

As a mentality to take into a heat, it was super-basic, but I liked it. *It's not so ridiculous*, I thought. I figured I could probably pull off two or three half-decent rides. On the other hand, any display of stamina, sustained effort . . . that's what I knew in my bones was beyond me.

I WAS DRAWN IN Heat 12 – the last on the program – with Ethan Ewing and Sebastian Zietz. The swell was medium-sized at three to four feet, just over head-high. A fast-moving point break, Snapper's wave isn't conducive to aerial tricks. The best way to accrue points is to put together four or five turns in a sequence.

I went down on my first wave – a big plunge out of the lip of a floater. Apparently, there were a lot of concerned 'oohs' and 'aahs' on the beach because I fell hard, but I was unhurt. I simply reminded myself of the goal: *Stay on your board*. I might have put an expletive in front of 'board'.

I didn't have time to worry, anyway. I'd ended up on the inside where this nice little double-up arrived. It was just under head height with a nice speed to it. I took it, and it let me get off six or seven turns that were all clean and crisp. My reward was a score of 8.23, the foundation of a winning tally.

I'd barely regained my breath when another tempting wave loomed before me. While I didn't have priority, Ewing and Zietz let the wave go, so I pounced. Again, I strung together half-a-dozen turns – big backside efforts – to earn a 6.27. I had my back-up score – and the heat was only fifteen minutes gone.

I could afford to coast for a while. All being well, that thought wouldn't occur to me, but the fall and two taxing rides had drained me. As unfit as I'd been at any time in my life, I needed to regroup. While both Ewing and Zietz were more than capable of overhauling me, a wave of fatalism swept over me. I'd done what I'd set out to do – complete two waves. Now, I figured, I'd surrender to the will of the universe.

For five minutes I just floated, regenerating, before paddling into the biggest wave of the heat. It doubled up and offered a generous section that allowed me to relax into my work. I got off three turns, then felt my body tightening up. From there, my movements felt forced. If you have an eye for surfing, you'd have seen I was gassed, and the judges would have seen it. But those first three turns were excellent and I came flying off the bottom and did a big carve. Because I'm tall, I can open up my body a lot and I did three more massive turns in a row, then I got a fourth that was nice. By then I was spent, man. My knees were wobbling, and it was all I could do to stay upright until, performance complete, I exited off the back of the wave.

My score: 8.60.
My total: 16.83.

The heat was mine. And by winning it, I'd earned a day off: I was straight through to Round 3.

Afterwards, as well as being dog-tired, I was dizzy from all the unfamiliar up-and-down motion. I checked in with Paul via Skype; he was thrilled for me. My symptoms didn't surprise him, and he green-lit me to compete again in two days' time.

That night and into the next day, I rode an emotional seesaw, variously crying, shaking and laughing. To my mind, it defied logic to be competing and winning again after the depths I'd plumbed. On the upswings, I'd rarely felt so great. I felt like me again. I'd reattached to the me I knew, the me I could live with.

'You've done it once,' Micro said. 'You can do it again.'

Maybe, I thought. But if I was going to advance past my next heat, I'd have to do it without practising for two days. I didn't have the strength.

MY NEXT OPPONENT WAS none other than Mick. A tall order, and yet I felt a strange sense of comfort in competing against someone I knew. Mick was more than that, of course: on top of all our other contact, he was one of the guys who'd carried me out of the Rip Curl House to the ambulance.

It was a morning heat, which was good, because these days I felt freshest early. The waves were slightly bigger and cleaner than they had been, offshore and rolling through – another plus.

'Just take off and stay on your board,' said Micro.

Yes. *Stay on your board.* My new mantra.

Would Mick have felt any sympathy for me? During the heat, not a chance. He's too competitive for that. A cold-eyed, aggressive frontrunner, he came out the image of a man on a mission. He took the first wave and belted the living daylights out of it for a 7.83. Then he hopped onto the jet ski to be taken straight back out, wearing an expression that said: *That was just my first blow – you have plenty more coming.* He's so good, Mick. You know he's going to score 14 points minimum with his eyes closed. The quality of wave doesn't matter to him; he'll find a way to score on anything. And he'll never beat himself. To get past him, you need to surf your tail off. You need to respond to his salvos.

Which, somehow, I did. I took a wave that was bigger than his, considerably bigger, and rode it nicely, making some big turns out the back before slipping off at the end.

No sooner had I got us level-pegging than Mick launched again, notching a 5-point back-up.

Stay on the board. Pick well and stay on the board.

Ten minutes in, I went again and pulled off another bunch of turns. On one, I blew the whole back of the board out of the water, brought it around and straight back up for a vertical snap. I was too tired to finish well, but an untidy finish doesn't necessarily bother the judges unduly. My luck was in: they awarded me an 8.1. Once again, I'd amassed a solid total early before my inevitable petering out. It was my only hope.

Then, more good fortune: an ocean lull. Needing a 7.28 to pass me, Mick had nothing to work with for ten minutes. Finally, with the clock ticking down, he jumped onto a double-up and belted it. It was small but peeled perfectly, and Mick got off two colossal turns before pulling into the barrel. It would have felt good in there, but the thing is, judges tend not to be enamoured with barrel-surfing when the wave is on the puny side. If Mick had stayed out the front and just reeled off turns, I have no doubt he'd have scored what he needed. As it was, he came up fractionally short. I won the heat by a margin of 0.1.

The beauty of Mick was that he could spend thirty minutes trying to crush you, but when the hooter sounded and you were ahead, he was all good grace. He paddled over and hugged me, wishing me all the best. He also read my eyes, which said: *I can't believe I just beat you.*

I had to surf twice that day – Round 4 was a three-man, no-loser heat. If I won it, I'd have skipped Round 5, but I didn't. I was pipped by Connor O'Leary in a low-scoring affair.

Predictably, my father had stopped talking about me winning the event. Once a competition starts, he zeroes in on the process. And that process was simple. I cocooned myself in my borrowed pad with Kita and Vali. I kept my phone mostly switched off and conversation to a minimum. I channelled what limited energy I had into caring for Vali and found that calming. While Kita was excited about me winning heats, I had to lasso her enthusiasm.

'I just can't entertain any of this talk,' I said.

Micro, meanwhile, was still telling me to stay on my board and 'go for a surf'.

I rang Paul to report I was still in contention.

'Just keep going,' he said. 'And let me know if some of the backlash gets too much to handle.'

MY ROUND-5 ADVERSARY WAS Conner Coffin, a friend and Rip Curl teammate from Santa Barbara, California, who'd stayed with me in the past on the South Coast. The conditions were awful – choppy and sloppy.

'This plays into your hands,' Micro enthused. 'There aren't going to be many opportunities. This won't be a test of stamina. If you can stay on your board and get a couple of big turns away, you'll be in the hunt.'

I believed Micro. Wave selection would be paramount. Although it would be all rubbish to choose from, some waves would be less rubbishy than others.

While staying locked in the present, I became aware that not only were my strength and belief growing, but my surfing brain was firing up, too. And strangely, I didn't feel a trace of pressure. Having come this far, I'd already overachieved. I'd surprised everyone, except maybe my father.

Against Conner, I vowed to raise my output. All up, I caught six waves. Conner caught ten but couldn't match my best two scores, and I edged him by half a point, leading from the get-go.

I was through to the quarterfinals, where the cream had risen to the top: Kelly, Medina, Florence and Ferreira were all there. My opponent, however, was O'Leary again – a rookie from Sydney's Sutherland Shire. I'd watched Connor surf when he was a kid, noting a goofy footer with prodigious talent. *This kid is going to be amazing*, I'd thought. At a comp I attended as a spectator, I bumped into his mum, a hardcore surfer just like Connor's dad. I'd seen her around a lot over the years.

'I think your son's going to be on the tour pretty soon,' I told her. 'He's got what it takes.'

I reckon I was the first person to say that to her, and she couldn't have looked more pleased. Connor arrived on the tour in 2017 as a solid, straight-shooting bloke and ferocious competitor.

The conditions for our heat were tricky, and we spent the first half of it falling and blundering. All the action came towards the end when I was leading by a whisker. He climbed on a wave, I followed him on the next one, and we surfed our respective waves all the way down the point. I could hear the crowd cheering his effort and suspected he'd achieved the score he needed. Thus, my do-or-die mission was to regain the lead on this wave.

I can't say I surfed my wave any better than Connor surfed his, but, crucially, mine was bigger, giving me a little more to work with. I executed some big backside turns, some carves and a floater, all nicely linked together, and won the heat by half a point.

By the way, Connor kicked on from there, finishing Top Ten in 2017 and claiming Rookie of the Year, as I had seven years earlier. But at Snapper, it was me advancing to the semifinals.

NO REST FOR THE wicked. I had a little over an hour to prepare for Medina, who'd won this event in 2014. Back I went to the penthouse, where I sat quietly, happy yet incredulous that my run was continuing. In the space of a few days, my surfing had transformed. Gone was the stiltedness of my early heats, replaced by a style you might call free-flowing. I didn't have to be a robot anymore following a single command: stay on your board. I could let loose.

'Enjoy every minute of being back in this world again,' Micro told me before I paddled out.

I took a fall early. Nothing to worry about. Medina started fast and scored respectably. I chipped away and led narrowly with eight minutes left, when Medina began a long ride down the point that would have scored well had he not come unstuck in the chop. Time was running out for him. I let him have a wave, jumping on a better one behind it that doubled up beautifully. I got off two big, vertical turns then a carve, at which point it doubled up again and all I needed to do was continue the show, to keep the turns and snaps coming all the way to the end of the point, where I raised my arms. It was funny: it was the semifinals and that was the first wave I'd claimed, which tells you the extent to which I'd been simply trying to survive until then.

I scored big, leaving Medina needing a 9-point ride. While he's someone you write off at your peril, that task proved impossible. I mean, just pinch me, please: I was through to the Big Dance.

35

MY FOE IN THE FINAL, held that same afternoon, was Wilko. It would be the battle of the buddies. In the hour or so between our semis and the decider, we were mostly in each other's company, revelling in the fact that our fortunes had collided.

Everyone knows that a great one-on-one contest requires contrast – in the backgrounds, styles and personalities of the combatants – and ideally at least some smidgin of ill-feeling. Matt and I could deliver on none of those criteria. My father and Wilko's dad Neal had been mates for fifteen years. Wilko and I had lived parallel lives, travelling around in our vans as juniors, with our dads at the wheel. We'd slept over at each other's houses. We were both tall and lean goofy footers, both sponsored by Rip Curl, and both coached by Micro.

Wilko had seen me close to death in the Rip Curl House; he'd visited me in hospital in Hawaii; he'd visited me at home on the South Coast. When I'd become more mobile, I'd stayed at his house in Byron Bay, where we'd hung out together at the beach and I'd tried to paddle out on a longboard.

This was a tour final, but both of us were too stoked to be nervous. In the locker room, we helped ourselves to some guy's wax and waxed our boards together.

'Can you believe this?' he said.

'No way.'

And I couldn't either. On any number of counts, what was happening felt surreal.

Micro was looking like a mastermind with two of his athletes in the first final of the year – Wilko as the defending champion, me on the comeback. In yesteryear, it was one surfer per coach. But the pool of coaches has shrunk, and now they tend to have stables of four or five athletes. Coaching surfing at the pro level is an extremely time-consuming job that can rip you away from your family for up to ten months of the year, and the pay reeks unless you have multiple charges. At Snapper that year, Micro and his wife Jemma had two little kids with another one on the way. You don't become a surf coach to get rich. You do it for the love and betterment of the sport.

'Boys, you know the point,' Micro told Wilko and me. 'You know the line-up. You know what's doing out there. You know your own strengths. Both of you go out there and do your individual thing. But don't treat it like a cosy little mates' heat, where you go easy on each other. Treat it with the respect it deserves.'

I felt Micro spent just a little bit more time with me than he did with Wilko in that emotion-filled hour. I reckon he figured that Wilko, healthy and fully fit, could look after himself.

'You've come this far,' he told me, when it was just the two of us. 'Be proud of what you've achieved and enjoy the moment.'

Mum, Dad, my siblings – my whole family was there, while Wilko had his partner Anna, his dad and a bunch of mates in his corner. I'm pretty sure his dogs were there, too.

The conditions were dismal – as messy as a teen's bedroom. I grabbed the first wave, felt sharp but scored insignificantly; Wilko reciprocated. We were both waiting for the waves to improve.

Wilko went again, executing a few nice turns on a wave that carried him through to the inside, where it doubled up cleanly and spurred him to try a big blow-tail. But he fell off the back, keeping his score in the 3s. I responded with a wave that I surfed down the point, doing bits and pieces along the way, earning a 5 flat. Fifteen minutes in, the best thing was I felt neither stiff nor tired. In the earlier heats, I'd needed to do the bulk of my scoring early in the piece before I flagged. By the final, I felt capable of a late strike. I could hear the crowd responding to our efforts but, in truth, hamstrung by the conditions, Wilko and I were delivering less than riveting entertainment.

Despite our friendship, we hadn't exchanged a word since we'd slipped on our rashies. That's the way it works. You may sit next to each other in the line-up, close enough to hear the other guy breathe. You may love him like a brother. But you don't speak during competition.

With fifteen minutes left, the action picked up. Wilko threw down the gauntlet with a 6+ ride. I needed to lift. I hopped on a wave and set up for a blow-tail reverse. It's a favourite manoeuvre of Wilko's, but I felt ready to push myself by attempting a crowd-pleaser. As far as I'd come at this event, I hadn't done any spinning, but that was about to change. I blew my fins around and did a full 360, recovered and resumed surfing the wave. My score wasn't huge but the effect it had on my confidence was. It had been a year and a half since I'd done a turn like that.

Wilko got another wave with a big, clean face and smashed it. He now led by 1.5 points, a lead I narrowed with a ride that featured a couple of carves.

I jumped out the back and spied a big set coming. Wilko had priority, but I made like I was going for the first wave, selling it to him as though it were something unmissable. Wilko took it, I bailed, and Wilko's ride was solid but ended in a fall.

The second wave of the set was all mine. All day, the second waves had been better. This one had doubled up better. It was the turning point of the heat because my wave gave me three turns out the back, and through the inside I got off two more big turns then finished the wave on my feet. My score: 8.33. I was leading with just a few minutes left.

The waves went south, and Wilko had nothing to work with as the minutes turned to seconds. He tried one but it was hopeless.

Right at the death, something half-decent arrived. I had priority and I used it. The wave came to nothing and then I heard the blast of the hooter. It was over. I'd won.

Wilko paddled over to me, and we looked at each other. My eyes screamed disbelief: *How did that happen?*

The WSL's on-air analyst, Strider Wasilewski, pulled up next to us on the back of a jet ski. Typically, only the winner gets interviewed, but there was nothing typical about this day.

Wilko told Wasilewski he'd have loved to have won, but he was happy for me. 'Owen has made me cry five times this week.' The sight of me in the Rip Curl House that day at Pipe was the gnarliest thing he'd ever seen, he said, then turned to me. 'If anyone had to beat me, I'm so glad it's you.'

Mikey and Tyler reached me while I was wading ashore and lifted me onto their shoulders. A bit later, Dad approached me in his ten-year-old clothes, looking daggy and scruffy. He grinned broadly and hugged me. He didn't say, *I told you so.* Not his style.

Kita's reaction was priceless. Corey photographed her as she embraced me with Vali pressed to her side. Kita is screaming in delight. *We did it!* That was the mood. *We've somehow made it back. Those many months of shit we went through together? They're behind us now. And we have something to show for them.*

I called Paul. We compared notes on our shared sense of astonishment.

'To be honest,' he said, 'I expected you to pull out after the first heat.'

At the end of the call, we agreed I should turn up for the next event, at Margaret River in Western Australia.

Tim and Mikey wanted to celebrate into the night and had made a booking at nearby Rattlesnake nightclub, but I was wrecked. I was no chance of going. They didn't care. They had the afterparty without me, and Wilko went along and kicked up his heels while I lay in bed, basking in the thrill of an outlandish victory.

I still don't know how I won that event. Since qualifying for the tour in 2010, I haven't arrived at a comp in worse shape than at Snapper Rocks in 2017. Low on fitness, practice and confidence – in poor health, really – I made it through seven rounds against the best surfers in the world. Sure, I had some luck with timely waves and close results falling my way, but you don't fluke a tour win, I can promise you. They're devilishly hard to come by. Snapper '17 still feels less like a victory than a delightful and mind-boggling shock, which once happened to a guy who might have been me.

In the years since, I've often tried to re-create the same headspace that I had at Snapper. But it's an odd headspace to be groping for because it was essentially survival mode. I can assume only that there must have been something valuable in the sheer simplicity of Micro's strategy – the notion of trying merely to stay upright, keep my feet on my board – all the while doing no more than *having a surf*, not so much competing as pleasure-seeking, unconcerned (or less concerned than usual) with results.

But it's puzzling. The truth is, you don't know what will work and when. If there were a magic formula, winning would be simple. You'd be unbeatable. Or you'd be Kelly Slater.

36

THE NEXT MORNING, I was struggling. Exhaustion and agitation had swamped the euphoria of the night before, and I was no help in organising our departure. Nonetheless, I didn't contemplate pulling out of the next leg of the tour, just a few days away.

The first thing that struck me at Margaret River was the size of the swell: it was big, about ten feet, dwarfing what I'd faced at Snapper. You need to understand that I wasn't fearing these heavier waves consciously. My mind wasn't linking what had happened at Pipe with the anxiety I felt now as I gazed out to sea. In my mind, I was the old me, the guy who relished bigger surf. My body, however, knew better. My chest felt tight, my breathing was shallow and my sleep was shot.

Somehow, I still performed, reaching the quarterfinals. But in my heat against the Gold Coast's Jack Freestone, I fizzled, catching just two waves for a meagre tally of 5.50. Towards the end of the heat, while I was still in contention, the fin dropped out of my board, killing my chances. But I was glad it did. That's right: more notable than my insipid performance was my reaction to losing. I was relieved because I couldn't take the stress anymore. Sitting on my board against Jack, I'd decided that even if I jagged the win, I'd withdraw from the event. Ultimately, that wasn't necessary, but I'd have done it – I'd have walked, as sure as the dawn.

Maybe I should have skipped the next stop, Bells Beach. Both Paul and Micro could sense I was running on vapours. But the competitor in me couldn't countenance pulling out, without first gauging what was possible.

In the lead-up, I was hard to live with – moody, teary and obsessive. Kita would have needed all her patience not to clock me. I was getting fixated on things, like not being able to free-surf because I was too weak.

'It's not fair,' I kept saying, as though there were something Kita could do about it.

One day, we were supposed to be catching up with friends, but I was so wigged out that we ended up staying home, where I hardly said two words to Kita the whole afternoon.

Somehow, I managed to win my first heat – and win it well. But afterwards, I asked to see the onsite doctor.

'I've lost confidence in what I'm supposed to be doing,' I told Micro. 'I shouldn't be here. It's too much.'

The doctor examined me – my heart rate, blood pressure, my pupils' reaction to light – and tried to reassure me that I was okay. He and Micro counselled me to the effect that I had more to gain from pressing on and staying in the comp than from picking up my board and heading home to fret and mope.

I left the medical room, thinking, *All right, I'm struggling but I'm not in any danger. My brain is just backfiring a bit. It's a question of grit.*

But no sooner had Micro and I swung our attention to the next heat – against Bede, by then only fifteen minutes away – that I broke down. Wept like a jilted schoolgirl.

'Man, what am I doing here?' I sobbed.

Micro stepped up. 'Mate,' he said, 'you might not know who you are, where you are or what you're doing, but every time you've paddled out for a heat, you've known what to do. You know how to surf. You can surf better than anyone and you don't even surf. It's the one thing your brain knows how to do, even if you don't know what your name is.'

I took solace in those words. *Micro*, I thought, *you're right*. The TBI, the tortuous recovery, the numerous relocations, the family tensions, Vali's arrival . . . why had I thought I could absorb all of that and return to the tour without a hiccup? For a year, I'd barely seen a soul. And now, in the space of a month, I'd competed in three locations. I was overloaded.

As Micro had implied, although I was mostly staggering about in the dark, surfing could be my crack of light. I'd been doing it since I was five. If I knew nothing else, I knew how to surf. So I walked, chin up, into the light.

More accurately, I ran into it. Because the clock was ticking. I was running late. Normally, you'd sit with your coach and study the waves for an hour before competing. But I'd lost all that time in a meltdown. Micro grabbed a security guard to help us weave through the crowd on our way to the beach. We were going full pelt as Micro fielded calls from officialdom demanding to know where I was.

But I made it. And I paddled out. Against Bede, I competed in a state near to bliss, notching an untouchable score of 17.54.

It was another turning point. Since coming back, I'd had plenty of wins, but I hadn't felt nearly as in command as I did against Bede. And that was because I'd deemed the ocean my safe place. I knew surfing and waves like I knew nothing else. I knew the fundamentals of heat management as well as anyone. These were the constants in my otherwise chaotic life.

I didn't know exactly how to be a partner, father, social being and all these different things, but I knew how to surf and how to win a heat. And with that new clarity of thought, I'd paddled out for my latest test and smashed it. You can watch the heats at Snapper and see I was suboptimal. I was winning but I was robotic. Against Bede, I surfed like the surfer I'd dreamed of being one day as a kid.

When I came ashore from my win, someone – a journalist, I suppose – asked me a question that I didn't know how to answer. Again, I broke down. The funny thing was, I was crying but I was okay with crying. I didn't know what I was doing in my life but on the water, I was in control. Surfing was going to pull me through. I ended up losing at Bells to Mick in a high-scoring heat, but with the psychological leap I'd made, I felt excited about the rest of the year.

COME JULY, PAUL ADVISED me to travel earlier than usual to Teahupo'o and to practise in big-wave conditions ahead of the event. In hindsight, my neurologist understood better than I did that the anxiety I'd been experiencing in the presence of a large swell could be sheeted home to my Pipe catastrophe.

He suggested that I should consider taking melatonin to help with my ongoing sleep trouble.

But even though, sure enough, my anxiety returned in Fiji in the form of bouts of shaking, I continued to baulk at a pharmaceutical solution. *Why cave now?* I thought. My only concession to my jangling nerves was a kava supplement. From the time of my first heat to my elimination in the quarterfinals, I was mostly a nervous wreck, and yet each time I paddled out, I performed.

Without placing highly at any of them, I did better psychologically at the next three legs – in California, France and Portugal – but back at Pipeline for the season-ender, I floundered. The surf ceased to be my sanctuary. In my Round 1 heat against the veteran Josh Kerr from Tweed Heads and Kanoa Igarashi, a Japanese-American whiz-kid, I froze. I barely took a wave. I was catching cold in the line-up from sheer inactivity. A miserable tally of 3.37 from two 1-point-something rides should have told me everything I needed to know about my mental state. But still, I couldn't put two and two together.

You'd assume that I was saying to myself, *Shit, these waves are huge! I'm back at this place that almost killed me and I'm about to get hurt again. Except this time, I'm not going to make it.* But that wasn't happening. I was simply feeling the anxiety like a pernicious force of unknowable origins. I had such strong rhetoric playing in my head – that I preferred big waves and surfing was my sanctuary – that I was incapable of paying attention to context.

At Snapper, I'd weighed eighty-two kilograms – on the light side for me. At Pipe, I was down to seventy-six. And right there was another sign of the strain I'd endured back on the tour. Though I should have probably quit after the debacle of Round 1, I showed up for a make-or-break heat against Ewing. My score in that heat looks better – 10.77 – but I was still terrible and lost. I forced myself to get on a couple of waves but spent most of the half hour letting great waves go. I scored a couple of 5s, but I was waving goodbye to 8s. Ewing, in contrast, had a go. He took off on much better waves than I did, and it was only errors of execution that kept the scores close. Really, there was one guy surfing out there and one guy cowering.

Back on the beach, my head was down. But if I could have viewed the season through a wider lens in those moments, I might have felt satisfied, even delighted, with an overall sixth-place finish.

That evening, in the Rip Curl House, my teammates screened a little film they'd made, in which they took turns congratulating me on coming back to the tour and doing so well. I cried through that tearjerker. I was also joyful for Tyler, who won the women's world title for the second year in a row.

37

IF I WAS LOOKING for positives – and I was – I'd say that something else pleasing about 2017 was that I got through it without suffering a concussion. That had a lot to do with having barely free-surfed, which is when you take more risks. Now, in the off-season between my comeback year and the start of the 2018 tour, I resolved to train harder, to push my limits. The result: I sustained another head knock.

As was my custom, I'd taken a break after Pipeline that extended into the middle of January; my birthday on the sixteenth is my signal to fire up again. One morning, while surfing at Kirra Point, just north of Snapper, I fell off a wave and hit my head on the ocean floor. I suspect I lost consciousness momentarily, but I had enough of my wits about me to wade out of the drink and stumble along the sand to where Kita, Vali and Tyler had set up camp.

The women took one look at me and their faces whitened. I had blood on my forehead and a thoroughly vacant appearance, apparently, as though an alien spacecraft had just returned me to earth. They took me to Mikey's house nearby, where I was assessed by the WSL's medical director Chris Prosser, who made the call that I should go to hospital. *Here we go again,* I thought.

Watching me battling dizziness and nausea and struggling to find the right words, Kita was distraught with rekindled memories and fresh fears. Fortunately, at the hospital, I felt quite a bit better within a few hours, but was kept in overnight for observation.

Typically, Paul found an upside to this latest incident when I spoke to him from my hospital bed the next day.

'No, this is a good thing,' he said.

'How so?'

'It shows you that you can get rag-dolled and recover. Knocks are going to happen in your sport, and you need to know your brain can withstand them.'

This latest concussion was only mild, he said, but the symptoms were severe because my brain was highly sensitised, primed to overreact to trauma. In time, it would settle.

'Go back to your routine,' he advised. 'If things fall apart, take a break and resume it the next day.'

So, that's what I did. It was probably six weeks before I felt completely better, at which point I added a new form of training to my regimen. I'd started doing these online sessions with a Hawaiian trainer named Kid Peligro, who calls himself a Ginástica Natural instructor. His style of workout is sequences of bodyweight exercises that flow from one to the next; there are a lot of animal-type movements targeting mobility, flexibility and strength. It felt like I was training a little like a pro again, instead of just getting by on an everyman level of fitness.

I still hadn't resumed weight training, though. I'd tried it once and it was a disaster, making me feel dizzy and zapped, as well as sore and sorry for days. Paul suggested the weights could wait a while longer.

I started thinking more about the brain and concussion and how surfing, which I'd never thought of as a high-risk sport, despite my storied medical history, was more dangerous than I'd realised or wanted to admit. Because I was the TBI guy, several surfers – particularly big-wave chasers – were asking me what my symptoms had been following my various knocks. When I told them, they'd say, 'Oh, that's what I had after I wiped out at [someplace].' It seemed like I was helping them make sense of their historic mental struggles.

Kita was ambivalent about my drive to keep competing. She knew I lived and breathed surfing, but there was also a limit to the punishment I could withstand and her capacity to watch me suffer. I think she was also shocked that all this stress around health and safety would be part of a surfer's world. She'd imagined surfing as bronzed, laidback dudes engaged in a beautiful, harmonious relationship with the sea. What was all this trauma? After all, she hadn't given her heart to a UFC fighter or BASE jumper.

IN FEBRUARY, I MADE another reassessment of my boards. I'd had some fine results with JS Industries, but now I was struggling to find a board I felt comfortable on. At first, my troubles were mystifying. But in time, it became clear the issue was my new and inferior body: JS's higher-volume boards simply weren't the perfect match for me anymore. I couldn't push my weight through them the way I once did, partly because of my lower bodyweight and partly because I was lacking strength since I wasn't training with weights. As a result, I found myself continually skimming across the top of waves, instead of making indents from which I could establish a sense of balance and control.

Anyway, I got hold of some old Horizon boards and took some advice from another shaper, who reduced all the volumes. I went back to JS to do the same, but we failed to hit the mark a couple of times. I then received some promising boards from DHD (Darren Handley Designs). Darren is a renowned shaper based at Burleigh Heads. DHD uses a foam for its boards that makes them more suited to the lightweight surfer, whereas JS products are more suited to the powerful surfer, which is what I used to be.

Because I was getting a livelier feeling from the DHD boards, I found myself in a quandary. I had a great relationship with JS, on whose boards I'd had good results in 2017 and a decent start to the new year, with quarterfinal placings at Snapper and Bells. But in May, when the tour moved to Indonesia for a double-header, I made the switch.

Now, anyone in the know will tell you that changing boards midseason is madness. The time and effort involved in adjusting to new boards and modifying your lines virtually preclude a switch outside of off-season. But I was able to do it while maintaining a high level of performance, which speaks volumes for the boards more than anything else.

But first, I need to back-track to Snapper. I'd started my campaign on fire there, scoring big points on my way to a quarterfinal against the veteran Adrian 'Ace' Buchan from

Avoca Beach. The night before, this big swell came through –
a cyclone swell – and the WSL moved the next day's action
from a washed-out Snapper along the beach to Kirra, the scene
of my latest knockout.

I didn't go out for a surf that morning because I'd talked
myself into thinking I didn't need to. Little did I know, I was
walking down a track towards choking. Because when I got
my first look at the size of the waves – up to eight feet – all this
anxiety came flooding in.

'Just catch your two waves,' Micro advised. 'You know how
to barrel-ride.'

Sure. But having paddled out to the line-up, I froze again.
I wasn't jockeying for position; I wasn't getting underneath the
better waves. What I was doing was a pretty good impression
of a piece of flotsam. My total score was embarrassing: 2.50.
I'd have backed Vali to top that. Up against an Ace, I'd surfed
like a joker.

Afterwards, I was kicking the sand with frustration, still
blind to the cause of my mental frailty. Again, I know that
seems hard to believe. But as someone who'd relished big waves
for so long, I couldn't concede a fear of them, even to myself.

Was my ego getting in the way of a clear-eyed view of things?
You bet. No one wants to be the surfer who's gun-shy of the
big stuff. Taking on the larger waves is a bit of a hero thing,
and I'd prided myself on that based on all the big waves I'd
charged in the past. That's who I thought I was: The Charger.
I'd built my identity on it. So, yes, I was in denial. *No way am
I intimidated! No way am I scared!* That's how I was thinking.
I've got the skill, so why can't I do it out there? Why am I not

winning in these conditions? I've been better than most of these guys in these conditions my whole life. But I just can't get it done.

I wasn't thinking about it at the time but now, I can imagine that my fellow pros could see the truth. And that hurts. That hurts like a wasp sting.

Between Snapper and Bells, I didn't address the psychology of what was going on. I had smart people around me who *wanted* me to address it, but I brushed the issue aside. I didn't want to know about it. I was too preoccupied with trying to tell myself that I was great, which I needed to do to continue my climb out of TBI hell. All my self-talk was about pushing forward, staring down challenges, ignoring setbacks. *Don't dwell. Don't loiter. Don't let your feelings take hold of you. March on.*

Something else happened during Snapper. I met a girl who was hanging around with Tyler. I remember thinking, *Wow, you're just like Tyler in the way you hold yourself and your no-nonsense, straight-up manner.* I assumed they were friends. But that wasn't quite right.

BELLS OFFERED ME A reprieve in the form of smaller waves that I surfed well to reach the quarters, where I was eliminated by Mick in his last appearance as a fulltime presence on the tour. Recent circumstances – his front-row seat for my brush with death at Pipeline, his brother's passing, his run-in with the shark – had dulled Mick's appetite for competition.

At Bells, the smoke cleared around Tyler's new companion. One morning, around the dining table at the Airbnb that Kita and I were sharing with Tyler, my sister seemed nervous. She seemed to have something she wanted to tell us.

And there was. Her new friend, she said, wasn't just a friend. 'She's my girlfriend.'

I'd never previously given a moment's thought to my sister's sexual orientation, but this made a certain sense. Tyler had dated guys in the past but, to be honest, I hadn't been madly impressed by any of them. I'd say to myself, *Well, he's not going to cut it.* Because Tyler has such a strong and solid character.

Like I said, Tyler seemed nervous about telling us, but so long as she was happy, I couldn't care less about who she was seeing.

'Yeah,' I said. 'And?'

Kita, meanwhile, was thrilled for her – thrilled that Tyler was in love.

Tyler had met her girlfriend back in March at a music festival. Their connection was instant, and they'd been inseparable from that first night. But the ensuing months were monumental for my sister; first, she accepted her sexuality and then she confronted the prospect of being an openly bi woman within surfing culture, which was notorious for its sexism and homophobia. I'd like to believe that surfing culture has changed, and I think Tyler would say that it has.

AT THE RIO PRO, Brazil, in May the waves got big and my issues resurfaced. Though I didn't experience the ignominy of my Snapper freeze-up, I felt rushed and jumpy in the ocean, too unsettled to perform.

The tour moved to Indonesia, where my new boards came out and, man, they made a difference. My placings of thirteenth and ninth were less important than how I felt in the ocean – reinvigorated. I was delighted with how things were tracking.

The fortnight in Bali was an important time for my family. As Tyler, Mikey and I sat on the beach one afternoon, my sister initiated another weighty conversation. She was burned out, she said. The way she was feeling, she didn't want to be here competing.

'Well, why don't you take a break?' I said. 'You don't need to show up to every event. Step back. Go and enjoy your life.'

It was good that Mikey was there. Only eighteen months separate him and Tyler in age, and Mikey's always had a free-surfer's mentality – the conviction that the joy of surfing trumps the pursuit of acclaim and riches under its banner.

'He's right,' Mikey said. 'Why don't you take off for a while? If you don't want to do this now, then go travelling.'

'Do something fun,' I said. 'Go to America. Do Disney-world or something.'

'You know you can win these events,' Mikey said. 'You know it, we know it, everyone knows it. You've got two world titles. You can win again when you're ready.'

Tyler was taking everything in without saying much. Finally, she said, as much to herself as to us, 'I just haven't stopped for so long.'

She did stop, though. That event in Indonesia turned out to be her last one for a while. The tour moved on to South Africa, but instead of competing, Tyler went with Mick on a Rip Curl–sponsored trip to an undisclosed location in North

Africa, to seek out and surf this fast-barrelling wave touted as 'hidden' or 'secret' with no motive other than enjoyment. After that, Tyler came to Port Elizabeth, South Africa, where we both became crazily sick with different ailments.

I hadn't been feeling crash-hot during J-Bay. I'd lost my appetite. I'd eat a couple of mouthfuls and feel full, as though I'd ingested a three-course meal. Then when I lay down, it felt as though food was travelling back up my oesophagus towards my throat. This went on for a few days, during which I progressed to the final sixteen. In my last heat, however, I was throwing up while paddling out and had to withdraw.

I went to bed in my hotel room that night with a stomach-ache and a moderate case of diarrhoea. I awoke around midnight in agony, feeling like my abdomen was being ripped in two – it was scene from *Alien* stuff. I crawled outside onto the balcony, screaming and vomiting in this little neighbour-hood right on the point at Jeffreys Bay.

'Fletch!' I hollered. (This was Ryan Fletcher, my Rip Curl team manager.) 'Fletch!'

Fletch appeared on his balcony and took in the scene. 'Geez, what's going on?' He then went to wake up the WSL doctor.

An ambulance was called and the two of them loaded me into a car – I was so sick they'd decided we should meet the ambulance halfway, on the street somewhere. The intense pain had me in a panic, and I stuck my head out the window, yelling intermittently, as we sped into the night.

The paramedics decided against giving me analgesics. Based on my medical history – the TBI, specifically – and how

I was behaving, they suspected I was having a psychosomatic episode.

At the hospital, the emergency doctor pushed gently on my stomach. I all but leaped off the bed.

'You have a bowel obstruction,' he said.

'What?'

'You're blocked.'

'What do you mean? I've had diarrhoea.'

'Yes, but you've also had vomiting and reflux. It's a bowel obstruction.'

The initial treatment was a drip. *Please work*, I thought. But after fifteen minutes, there was no change. Then another, more senior-looking doctor showed up and addressed the first doctor: 'I'm giving you twenty minutes to unblock this or we're putting him straight into surgery.'

Mercifully, about ten minutes before this deadline, the drip started to work. I was discharged the next day, once tests had ruled out anything too sinister as causing the problem. I spent the next several days swallowing an awful concoction, a vile witch's brew, to get my system working properly again before Mikey escorted me home to Lennox Head.

No sooner had I come good than Tyler was being treated at the same hospital in Port Elizabeth. She seemed to have contracted some horrendous exotic virus that was causing shooting pains in her legs, full-body weakness and hallucinations, among other symptoms. She was diagnosed with influenza A, a potentially lethal strain of the flu. Her treating doctor prescribed her antibiotics and sent her on her way. Ten days later, her fever broke, and she flew home.

But then, Tyler stopped getting better; she started getting worse. She all but stopped eating and had barely the strength to climb out of bed. Crushing headaches, delusions and memory lapses set in. My indestructible sister felt physically broken. This went on for months before her condition was identified as post-viral syndrome – a mysterious, untreatable condition not unlike chronic fatigue syndrome.

Tyler would be off the tour until the final event of 2019, almost a year and a half after she caught the flu.

38

DOESN'T LIFE FEEL GREAT after you've shaken off an illness? I arrived in Tahiti in August 2018 raring to go, determined to put to rest the issues I'd been having in bigger swells. Funnily enough, the forecast for Teahupo'o during the event was for smaller-than-normal waves. Once upon a time, this would have disappointed me. Now, I could see – and feel – the upside. I was still at a place I loved with its made-to-order left-hand break, but I wasn't getting the big-wave anxiety that had been kicking the stuffing out of me. And though smaller than usual, the swell was still decent: wins would be built on barrels and turns rather than airs, so I felt like I was in contention.

As it turned out, I made it all the way to the final, where I faced Medina. I got the early jump on him, dropping into a barrel and scoring 6.5. Medina squared the ledger with a fluent ride, then edged ahead. The lead was mine again when I squeezed into a tight tube and managed to hold my feet in a ride that lacked the wow factor but was a feat of balance. With less than two minutes to go, I still led. Another title was close enough to taste.

On this day, waves had been arriving as well-spaced singles rather than in sets of two or three as normally happens at Teahupo'o. My plan was to use my priority to take the next substantial wave and deny Medina the chance to snatch the win. With 1 min 46 sec left on the clock, a wave popped up that Medina could have ridden to victory. It was a great wave – one of the best of the final – so I took it and owned it. As I did, I knew I was in the process of increasing my lead.

When the waves are smallish like they were that day, spectators can take their boats right up to the back of the reef for a close-up view of the action. Kita and Vali were there watching.

On finishing my ride, I turned my head to face the line-up, expecting to see a flat ocean. What I saw instead caused my heart to sink. Rolling towards me was a pearler of a wave – a wave that should not have existed. Then, unbelievably, Medina emerged from behind its curtain of water, exiting the barrel like a superstar. Later, I found out that the wave I'd taken was the first of a three-wave set. Medina had taken the third wave, the pick of the bunch.

I didn't need to wait for the scores. I knew I was sunk. I glanced over at Kita, who was yelling at me to paddle back out and go again. Though I couldn't help but admire her never-say-die attitude, time was up. The final scores were posted:

Medina: 13:50
Me: 12:07

Credit where it's due: Medina had seized his chance. It's one thing for an unexpected wave to materialise, another to produce a virtuoso ride with a title on the line.

'God gave me that last wave,' Medina told the media.

I must admit, that's what it felt like to me, too.

THAT SECOND PLACING WAS my best result for the year, during which I never surmounted my big-wave issues. At the Quiksilver Pro France in October, amid thumping beach-breaking barrels, I was skittish and couldn't position myself for waves that would once have had me salivating.

Later that same month, in Portugal, the waves were smaller than usual. Again I excelled, reaching the last four and narrowly missing the final after I fell on my last wave against Joan Duru from France. That was a spirit-crushing loss because it ended my world-title aspirations for the year.

Nonetheless, this time I thought I was ready for Pipe. I thought I'd put my problems there to rest. Alas, it proved to be another letdown punctuated by daytime jitters and sleepless nights, during which at least I could make myself useful when Vali woke up – which was often. My campaign ended in Round 2 against a fresh-faced Hawaiian wildcard, Seth Moniz. I caught the first wave and scored decently, but the way I rode it was telling: so conservative, so risk averse. I was into the barrel early and out first chance. By contrast, Seth's first wave was a palace-corridor barrel followed by a spectacular air reverse. For me, there was an added element of frustration attached to this loss, because had I made it to the next stage at Pipe, I'd have finished Top Five for the year instead of sixth. There's a big difference between fifth and sixth. Sponsors will find a little extra for their Top Five athletes, but no one talks about the 'Top Six'.

It was a strange year, all up. While I'd performed well at traditional big-wave venues – Tahiti and Portugal – it so happened that the waves there weren't big in 2018. Then at Pipe, I'd discovered I was still a headcase in larger swell, that the disaster of three years ago continued to cast its shadow over everything.

39

BY THE START OF 2019, Surfing Australia was well and truly gearing up for the Tokyo Olympics. Of course, no one knew that COVID-19 would delay the Games for a year. Surfing Australia hosted a two-day camp at its High Performance Centre in Casuarina for those surfers in contention for the national team. I showed up as Australia's No. 2. It turned out to be a humbling couple of days.

On day one, all the surfers were put through a series of fitness tests overseen by Chris Prosser. These included a standing jump for height, one-rep max lifts (the maximum weight you can lift for one repetition) for the squat and bench-press, and various endurance and flexibility tests. Before we started, I knew I was going to struggle.

I stood back for a while and watched the other guys flaunt their fitness. Mikey was among the group, as were Ace Buchan, Jack Freestone, Ryan Callinan and Wade Carmichael. It seemed like everyone besides me had come ready to rip and tear. I watched forlornly as guys jumped like frogs and squatted like Arnie.

But I couldn't watch forever. I started doing the rounds and was woefully unimpressive. At that stage, I still hadn't resumed resistance training; my weight continued to hover around seventy-six kilograms, which was too light for my height; and I lacked strength, stamina and suppleness. I'd been doing those Kid Peligro twenty-minute bodyweight sessions twice a week, but nothing else. I was so far removed from peak fitness, it was embarrassing. The other guys were putting me to shame – and so were the women. I was moving from one testing station to the next as though bound for the gallows.

One test was especially humbling. Chris had included it with me in mind. It was a test of equilibrium and balance. The exercises would have been a cinch for a brain-healthy person, but I was failing horribly. The testers were looking at me with puzzled expressions. *Why can't he follow the dot? Why is he losing his balance?* I was completely dysfunctional, but they didn't know why because they didn't know my backstory.

'Are you all right?' they were asking me.

No, I'm not, I thought. I felt dizzy and overwhelmed, and I started to lose track of where I was and what I was doing there. When I left the room, the testers chased after me.

'No, no, you'd better sit down,' they said.

I sat down. It was lucky I did, because I was groggy and faint. I felt like I was on a different planet.

Demoralised, I stayed in camp, moving from the testing to this lecture we were all supposed to listen to. I spent the whole time sprawled on the floor at the back of the room, half-asleep. Even though I'd made it back to the tour and finished sixth two years running, these tests had flattened me. They'd zeroed in on my weakest link.

My dismal results reached Chris. He called me when I was back home to discuss them, but I didn't want to talk to him.

Nothing was going to mess with the fragile story I'd been telling myself – that I was healthy, back surfing and doing fine.

A WEEK OR TWO after the debacle at Casuarina, and two weeks before the tour opener at Snapper, I was free-surfing off Lennox Point one morning when I took another wipeout. I'd gone up for this floater only for the wave's base to drop out suddenly, sending me crashing headfirst and unbraced into the flats. For a second, the world turned black.

When I came to, I floated on my back for a few minutes, scanning for damage. My neck was sore – a whiplash kind of sore – and I was winded. It was a few minutes before I could induce my arms to work properly.

Nonetheless, like the warhorse I'd become (in my late twenties!), I hauled myself out of the water, up the beach and into my car. On the short drive home, I asked myself two big-picture questions.

Have I proved my point?

How much more of this can I take?

That same afternoon, my neck was so stiff and sore that Kita ended up driving me to hospital, where I was scanned. A doctor told me there wasn't much wrong with it, just old damage. I was also told that my concussion was mild but, again, I was probably so sensitised to knocks, so anxious about them, that my body seemed to be over-reacting to this latest one.

Chris called again. This time, I was ready to unload.

'This is getting a bit hard for me, man.'

'I know,' said Chris. 'It's been tough. But I think we've got a solution for you. I want you to see this guy in Melbourne. There are lots of different improvements to be made.'

The guy turned out to be Brett Jarosz, a sports and exercise chiropractor with a strong practice interest in clinical neuro-science. I arranged to see him when I would be at Bells in mid-April for the second event of the year. If, that is, I was still competing by then.

ONE LATE AFTERNOON, I left Kita and Vali at home and parked at Lennox Headland. I sat in the car, looking out to sea. Then I called Tyler.

'I don't think I can do this anymore. I've done enough. I'm not in a good way.'

Tyler had been observing me since my comeback. Much of what she'd seen had disturbed her. It wasn't just the hesitant surfing and extra knocks – it was the sight of me. I still hadn't had a single good night's sleep since the accident, and I looked haunted and too thin. I looked like what I was: a guy who'd been carrying too much stress for too long; a guy at the end of his tether; a guy who was either nearly or completely burned out.

I talked to Tyler about how quickly my life had moved in the past two and a half years, and how I was struggling to keep up. For me, it was an unusual outpouring of realism and candour because, up until then, I'd been trying to project an image of being in control.

As I was speaking, I was aware that I hadn't opened up like this to Kita, to whom I felt a sense of duty as a man to be a provider. I wasn't ready to show her this level of frailty that had me on the brink of quitting the tour. I suspected Kita would eagerly support my withdrawal, and I didn't want that idea to be gaining momentum just yet. I preferred to keep that decision in my own hands. As a result, at home, I was withdrawn.

'I understand,' Tyler said when I'd finished. Whatever decision I made, she'd back me, she said.

Oddly, the effect of this conversation was to make me want to press on. I competed at Snapper dosed up on anti-inflammatories, and I went all right, finishing ninth.

Between Snapper and Bells, I thought I'd try for a sense of deep relaxation in a floatation tank. I clambered into one and had been lying there for ten minutes, feeling okay, when I became aware of water splashing on and around my face. *That's weird*, I thought. *I didn't know these contraptions were like spas.*

I went for a second session and the same thing happened, only this time, the splashing was more violent. That's when I realised what was happening: *I* was causing the turbulence. I was shaking like Elvis.

I HAD MY FIRST chat with Brett Jarosz at the top of the stairs at Winkipop, Bells Beach's little brother. I showed up flat, feeling sceptical that he or anyone else could help me.

I found myself face to face with a guy about my height – a little taller even – but he was thickset, maybe 110 kilograms. He looked more like a rugby player than the elite basketballer he used to be. Like me, he had longish blond hair, except his was wavy. He wasn't your typical-looking medico, if there's such a thing.

I told him about my experience in the floatation tank, how my body had rebelled. This led into my sleep problems.

'Oh yeah,' Brett said. 'Is it that every time you nod off, it's like you're being shocked awake? Startled by what feels like a jolt of energy in your head?'

Gosh. Now he had my attention. 'Yeah, yeah. Exactly!' I said. 'I'm starting to fade, and then . . . wham.'

'What's happening is that your brain is needing input,' Brett said. 'It's losing track of where it is in space and time, so it needs to shock one or more of your sensory systems back into play. When your brain is not in a good way, it needs a certain type of sensory input – vision, say – for orientation. It's shocking you awake so it can function properly.'

'Yeah, that's exactly what it feels like,' I said. 'The problem is, I'm basically awake all night.'

As Brett and I kept talking, it became clear that all the meditation I'd been doing hadn't been helping one iota. Meditation involves turning within and quieting sensory input; its effect on me was to induce those same jolts.

'So that's why meditation isn't helping,' I said.

Brett was winning me over. And he hadn't even assessed me yet – he was just jotting down what I was telling him about my symptoms and voicing a few preliminary thoughts. Every concussion is different, he told me. Sure, you'll have a headache when you're concussed, but the precise physiological cause of that headache could be any one of twenty different things.

'What about muscle spasms?' he said.

'Yep, lots of those,' I told him, with different types in different parts of my body.

Brett was able to describe the various types in detail.

Brett did a little therapeutic work with me during Bells, using an approach called Functional Neuro-Orthopaedic Rehabilitation to target the pain I'd been having in my back. I can't tell you exactly what he did – it felt like a form of exercise therapy to reactivate muscles in my glutes that had been slacking off. I had to hold uncomfortable positions for a minute or more. Whatever it was he did, I surfed well at Bells, losing eventually to Florence.

With Kita and Vali, I stayed on in Melbourne for two weeks in a rented apartment around the corner from Brett's clinic in South Yarra, so he could thoroughly assess me and begin treatment. I saw him every second day. On day one, I explained to him where the bleed had occurred in my brain – the left frontal lobe. Using his fixation stick, Brett could induce certain eye-movement patterns that would stress a particular part of my nervous system and cause me to enter a deep state of brain fog, or what Brett called 'extreme cognitive fatigue'. My head flopped forward until my chin was on my chest, my eyes rolled upwards and to the right, and I'd feel spaced out for the next few minutes. The truth is, though, just about every eye-movement pattern was having that effect.

When Brett was finished, he put one of his big hands on my shoulder, looked me square in the eye, and spoke some words I'll never forget.

'How the *fuck* are you surfing?'

'I'm guessing,' I said.

Brett dropped his head and took a step back. 'Fuck that,' he said. 'You're in waves of consequence, you're still one of the best surfers in the world and you're out there *guessing*? You can't be targeting the lip. I know you can't be.'

'That's right.'

By 'guessing', I meant that because I was struggling to look up at a wave without making myself weak, the timing of much of what I was doing in the surf was based on guesswork or intuition rather than vision. To a large extent, I was surfing blind.

A little later in the fortnight, the results of one test Brett gave me were striking. It was a computerised eye-tracking test – a more sophisticated version of what he had done with his fixation stick. Brett uses this test to determine if an athlete is ready to return to their sport. He measures your eye-tracking capacity then compares your result to an age-and-gender-matched cohort. Generally, Brett won't return professional athletes to the fray until they're in the ninetieth percentile. My result placed me in the fourteenth percentile. In other words, a big fat flunk.

This all may sound worrying to you – and fair enough – but at least now I felt confident that I'd found the right therapist for the next phase of my recovery. I figured that if Brett could identify what and where my problems were so quickly, then he'd also know how to fix them. So began an association that continues to this day.

When Brett arrived, I was fading fast. I wasn't keeping up with the progressions within surfing in terms of aerials. And my low weight was worrying me because there didn't seem to be a floor. As I told you, I'd come back to the tour at the start of 2017 weighing eighty-two kilograms and had shrunk to seventy-six by the end of that year. You'd think I would have started rebuilding after that, but I continued to hover around seventy-six and at times went lower. By 2019, I hadn't been eating properly for several years. It wasn't that I was devouring junk; I was just consuming ridiculously small portions for a tall athlete. I was seldom hungry and at times had to force myself to eat.

Brett attributed this to an underperforming autonomic nervous system, which includes the vagus nerve. This runs from your brain through your face and thorax to the abdomen, and regulates various functions such as heart rate, blood pressure – and digestion. My autonomic nervous system was so dysfunctional that I could barely digest food – thus my ordeal in South Africa.

Through testing, Brett identified other issues, too. Normally, when you stand up from a seated or lying position, your autonomic nervous system shuts certain valves to hold blood in your brain. That wasn't happening in my case, which resulted in a soaring heart rate and feelings of light-headedness. Brett diagnosed a condition known as POTS (postural orthostatic tachycardia syndrome) and made fixing that his top priority.

Ever since what happened to me at Pipe, I'd had to keep rethinking my conception of the brain. It was responsible for thought and calculation and contemplation . . . that all made sense. But what was it doing screwing with my heart rate and digestion – these physical processes that I'd assumed were independent of my grey matter?

'Everything is the brain,' Brett said. 'Everything is the nervous system. These things that you think of as happening automatically – breathing, heart rate, balance – they're all coming from your brain stem.'

At the end of that intensive period with Brett, while I was still in Melbourne, I had my first uninterrupted night's sleep for more than three years. I'd nodded off at about 10 pm and awoke at sunup. The same thing happened the following night.

I went home in early May with a bunch of instructions from Brett.

Don't free-surf.

Fine.

Work on stabilising your body's response to exertion by holding a certain heart rate while pedalling on a stationary bike.

Check.

Do this group of vestibular or balance exercises five to seven times a day.

Five to seven?

'The brain loves repetition,' Brett told me. 'To form and reorganise synaptic connections, we need to have focus, we need to have intensity and we need to have persistence.'

'Okay. What else?'

'Embrace sound,' Brett said. 'Use a rain app for sleeping and do guided rather than silent meditations.'

My floatation-tank experience had gone wrong because it was too quiet. It turned out that total sensory deprivation was the last thing I needed.

40

BACK HOME, IT OCCURRED to me that Brett might be able to help Tyler, who was still languishing with post-viral syndrome. By this stage, she felt like she'd dived down every rabbit hole in search of a cure, but nothing had done much good.

Between events, I'd travel to Melbourne to see Brett. During one session, I raised Tyler, explaining her condition as best I could. 'What do you reckon? In your wheelhouse?'

'Yeah, possibly,' Brett said. 'Post-viral syndrome can impact the brain stem and cerebellum. There might be something I can do.'

So, Brett assessed Tyler. Before long, he was treating both of us, sometimes in Melbourne, and other times in a Gold Coast hotel room into which he'd bring his various pieces of equipment. Under Brett's care, both Tyler and I felt we were improving. We enjoyed comparing notes on our treatment.

'How's yours going?' Tyler would ask.

'Amazing. I feel like I'm coming on in leaps and bounds. Yours?'

'Yeah, good. Really good.'

I can't describe how happy it made me that I'd put Tyler in contact with someone who could alleviate her suffering after so many strikeouts with other therapists. She'd been on the spot when I was at my nadir in Hawaii and now, in a small way, I'd been able to reciprocate. I felt like a good big brother, which beats the heck out of feeling like a burden.

In Indonesia and Brazil, while I didn't set the surf alight, I felt more at ease. I'd realised that, two-plus years into my recovery, I wasn't fixed and shouldn't hope to be fixed; I was simply on my way back to my old self.

In South Africa, things started to fall into place. A lot of Brett's therapy had been focused on the connection between my brain and heart rate; the latter was still responding abnormally to exertion, fluctuating unpredictably and sometimes alarmingly. When I started seeing Brett, it was going haywire when it hit 100 bpm. It might plunge to 80, then spike to 140 without any change in my level of exertion. The effect of this during heats was to stress and deplete me. Brett had me training on a stationary bike; the initial brief was to hold my heart rate at 90 bpm for twenty minutes each day. When I could manage that for a fortnight without backlash, I raised my heart rate by 10 bpm and repeated the process.

By the time I left for J-Bay, I'd built up to 145 bpm – and felt so much the better for it, even though Brett eventually wanted me training at 160 bpm. Previously, anytime I took a wipeout in competition, I'd be a mess – dizzy, discombobulated and disinclined to catch another wave. Now, I could take a fall and brush it off. I was more focused in the surf, more present. I felt like a new man – a man with a vision of his future, not merely the next five minutes.

In J-Bay, I realised that I wanted to get married. It was time to cement my relationship with Kita, the mother of my son and the love of my life. I saw asking Kita to marry me as another step towards reclaiming my autonomy. Since Pipeline, life had mostly felt like a ride on which I was a passenger. Now, I was ready to vacate the backseat and clutch the steering wheel with both hands.

In South Africa, having consulted various people, I purchased a diamond. Back in Australia, a jeweller attached it to a thin rose-gold band and I took the ring – along with Kita and Vali – to the next stop: Tahiti. Few of the other wives and partners made this trip – they feared the mosquitos or something – but it was Kita's favourite spot on the tour. She loved the simplicity of the Tahitian lifestyle, the warmth of the people and the house we always stayed in there. Sitting atop a hill, it's the only residence visible from the line-up at Teahupo'o.

While Kita and I had talked vaguely about tying the knot, neither of us had ever forced the issue, although Kita had said to me once: 'I'm not having another kid until we're married.' That could have been construed as a hint, I suppose.

Just before we flew to Tahiti, in August, I passed Brett's computerised eye-tracking test for the first time, recording a score that put me in the ninety-fifth percentile. This felt momentous. I was coming right physically and, hopefully, about to get engaged. It seems to me that so much of what we call happiness is really a sense of controlling your life's direction and momentum. Suddenly, I felt like a five-star general.

THE EARLY ROUNDS AT Teahupo'o played out in small surf and I advanced to the Round of 16 without incident. This was when I decided to move matters along with Kita. I wanted to do this properly – chivalrously – so late one night after Kita had turned in, I called her dad Nick to ask for his blessing. I was surprised to find that I was pressing the keys with trembling fingers. Kita and I had been living together for more than three years and were already parents; nonetheless, I was nervous as I took this all-but-irrevocable step towards making a lifelong commitment.

'Of course!' Nick said. 'Gosh, you're already part of the family.'

We were winding up the call when Nick had a thought.

'I saw the swell forecast,' he said. 'You've got some big surf coming.'

'Yeah, looks like it.'

I didn't tell Nick this, but I was shitting bricks. I'd been feeling calm and self-assured until a few hours earlier, but the forecast was for conditions that could eat you alive. At Teahupo'o, a swell out of the south is generally friendlier than one from the west, and this swell was all but straight west.

I was trepidatious, and yet this was a different reaction to what I'd been having previously to the prospect of big waves. That had been bodily rebellion mixed with denial. This was the opposite: no cramps, no spasms, but a recognition that I was scared. That's right: scared. *I'm scared of this monster swell that's coming. I don't want to get hurt.*

To my mind, this recognition was progress. I was now sufficiently in tune with my psychological state – with my fear – to ask myself a question: *What am I going to do about it?* And not just ask the question but also answer it: *I'm going to get myself a helmet that will give me some protection from these behemoths coming my way.*

Surfing or generic water-sports helmets did exist, but they'd been more in vogue twenty years earlier. Most of them were now tucked away in the storerooms and garages of leather-skinned old wave-riders. Tom Carroll, my boyhood hero, famously rode to victory in the 1990 and 1991 Pipe Masters wearing a Gath helmet. *Tracks* described him as 'looking like some kind of invincible wave warrior', and his 'glorious gouge in the '91 semifinal was one of the greatest manoeuvres of all time . . . as if the helmet emboldened him to perform the iconic turn'. What had led him to don the helmet, Tom revealed, was the fate of American Steve Massfeller, who crashed head-first into the reef at Pipe in 1983, fracturing his skull. With a plate in his head, Massfeller returned to competitive surfing but suffers ongoing sight, speech and memory issues. 'I knew him before and after and saw the impact it had,' Tom said. 'It's hard when you see someone change like that.'

I reached out to a few locals, asking whether they had a helmet I could borrow. After a few leads came to nought, I hit paydirt through a bloke named Ryan, a hard-charging amateur with whom I'd free-surfed numerous times.

'Come over,' said Ryan, who lived down the road from where Kita, Vali and I were staying.

Waiting for me at Ryan's was a white helmet in pristine nick. If Ryan had ever worn it, it could only have been in the bathtub. Like its skateboarding equivalent, a surfing helmet is closefitting, virtually a skullcap. The sides cover your ears and you secure it with a chinstrap. I tried it on. A perfect fit.

'Thanks, man.'

'Good luck tomorrow,' Ryan said. 'I'm jealous.'

Like I said, Ryan's a hard charger. Nothing fazes him.

That afternoon, I went for a paddle in a little swimming hole tucked away in nature that Kita and I love. For half an hour or so, I swam around and duck-dived, getting a feel for my new apparatus. With each passing minute, I became ever more convinced that I'd found the solution to my troubles. Tomorrow's waves were going to be colossal, but I no longer cared because now I had a helmet. If I happened to hit my head on the reef, I'd live to tell the tale. I felt more than just relieved. I felt confident, supremely so, as though I could do anything out there in a furious ocean.

As predicted, the swell was huge and menacing – the ugliest I'd seen at Teahupo'o. When it's from the west, it comes out of the channel, moves like the clappers and closes out like a slammed door, giving you only a split-second to exit a barrel before you're dumped onto dry reef.

Paddling out in my helmet, did I feel self-conscious? Not at all. I felt like I was taking back my life. As I saw it, the alternative was to die out there, which kind of erased any embarrassment. I got straight down to it, charging as hard as I had in years. Instead of assessing, weighing or discriminating, I took virtu-ally everything – the meaner looking, the better. I was like a kid again.

My opponent in the Round of 16 was Bourez. Back in 2015, when I'd taken those free-surfing trips to Tahiti, Bourez had been in the surf with me, as bold and busy as a Jack Russell. We had a strong, healthy rivalry. And in 2019, we contested a high-quality, high-scoring heat, a blow-for-blow exchange that came down to the last set. Man, he was primed for that heat, Bourez. I don't know what life-changing decision he'd just made, but he was surfing like he'd made a doozy. Between us, not a single set went unridden. Balls to the wall, we call it.

When the first wave of that last set arrived, Bourez and I looked at each other. I knew he was going to launch. Why wouldn't he? It was a beast of a wave and he had priority. But I knew this break – there'd be another wave just as good, if not better, right behind it.

I didn't need to watch my opponent to know he'd make the drop and get a score that would edge him in front. My task was clear: take the second wave and nail it. As I launched, I could hear the crowd celebrating Bourez's effort. I was too primed, too in the flow, to fail and in my white helmet, I rode my wave to another win.

Afterwards, my helmet was the focus of a lot of interest – both media and public. I started something that day, I believe. The dismantling of any stigma associated with protective headwear had been renewed. I have no doubt that many surfers of all abilities had considered wearing a helmet, but refrained for fear of how it might look or what it might say about their mettle. I became something of a spokesman for helmets and was happy to play that role. I wanted to show kids that helmets were cool and encourage parents to pop a couple in the car before family trips to the beach. I was the right surfer to deliver the message because surfing fans knew my story – no clear-thinking person was going to question the wisdom of me taking precautions around concussion considering my circumstances. For me, there was no turning back. In the years that followed, while I wouldn't wear a helmet in all conditions, any time I sensed danger, on it would go. Before long, some of my fellow pros followed suit, especially at Pipeline. A helmet has its limits, of course. It's going to be more effective at preventing lacerations and skull fractures than concussion. But it's *something*. It's definitely something.

The day after edging Bourez, I was back in the surf and still charging, notching a 10-point ride in a winning score of 19.07 against Jadson. I then beat Jordy Smith in the semis to set up another Teahupo'o final against Medina. By then, the ocean had calmed. I did feel slightly self-aware contesting the decider in a helmet, but not enough to dispense with it.

I made mistakes in that final. Trailing towards the end, I was furious with myself. But I had this moment of resolve while sitting out there: *No, this is my time! I've fought my way back from a TBI. I've done all this rehab. Nope, this is not your day, Gaby. It's mine.*

I drifted to the inside, which left Medina alone a little further out. A wave passed underneath him and loomed in front of me; that was my signal to go. And this wave barrelled. Deep inside it, I couldn't see the exit. When it spat, I was still entombed. Then an opening appeared, and even before I sped through it and into the light, I was yelling and self-exhorting like Lleyton Hewitt.

Though I'd done enough to take the lead, I wasn't finished yet. Without so much as pausing for breath, I jumped off the back of the wave and race-paddled back out. I was back in competitive-beast mode where I felt like the dominant force, not some convalescent also-ran. I took another wave underneath his priority and emerged from that one yelling again. I was back – a winner again. At Snapper in 2017, I'd won somehow but as a fragile competitor. When I reflect on the question: *When did I reclaim my life?* – the answer is not Snapper '17 but Teahupo'o '19. Snapper was incredible but – how do I put this? – it wasn't me out there. Teahupo'o, on the other hand, that was me.

I'd planned to propose on the day after the final, but I was so exhausted that I fell asleep during a trip to a waterfall and the moment passed. That left the next day. I organised with my Tahitian family – the family that owns the house we stay in – to take us out on their boat to a nearby island in the late afternoon.

Before we left, I grabbed the ring, which I'd had to hide from Kita the whole time we were there – no easy feat, believe me. She's into everything; she finds everything. My hiding place had been a pile of my dirty clothes, which I figured she'd regard as my problem. Fortunately, she did.

At our island destination, partially submerged by the high tide, the crystal-blue water was lit by the setting sun. I took aside the lady of the family, confided I was about to propose to Kita and asked her to capture the moment in a photo. Touched and thrilled, she started crying.

The ring box was shoved down the back of my boardshorts. Clutching Vali to her right side, Kita slipped her left arm around my waist as we stood in shin-deep water and smiled for the camera.

'Hey, I've got a question to ask you,' I said, before dropping theatrically onto one knee. 'Will you marry me?'

Kita made the same face she'd made at Snapper in 2017: an expression that blended equal parts shock, joy and excitement. She said nothing, just slipped the ring onto her finger – which I took as a 'yes'.

Thinking back, proposing in water was an absurd risk. If the ring had toppled out of its box, it could have been lost forever. At the time, however, that scenario didn't occur to me.

With the tour schedule being what it is, the wedding would have to be in January – the only issue was *which* January. Would it be January 2020 or 2021? My attitude was: *Why muck about?* I was becoming engaged to get married, not to be engaged for the sake of it. Kita saw things the same way.

In Tahiti, I'd reconnected with the audacious surfer I'd once been and committed to a life with Kita. At last, I felt as though the rough seas were behind me, and I could cruise for a while. I was wrong.

41

SOMETHING WAS UP WITH my father. I could feel it. He'd always been quirky, prone to the odd non-sequitur, but lately any conversation I had with him had become a test of self-control. I'd be trying to tell him something – maybe something to do with my schedule for the coming weeks – and he wouldn't get it. He wouldn't be able to follow it.

Worse was being a passenger when he was behind the wheel. He'd attempt these hair-raising manoeuvres, and when you said something like: 'Dad, what the hell are you doing?', he wouldn't have a clue what your problem was. For example, he might pull up behind a car at a Stop sign and become furious with the driver in front for having stopped. Then he'd swing out and try to get past, even if there was no room.

What sealed it for me that something was wrong was when he got done by a scammer. In his prime, my father was as street-smart as a New York gumshoe. Never in a month of Sundays would he have been taken in by some bogus scheme promising to triple your money. But Dad handed over a sizeable sum, then was chuffed to receive a phoney statement reporting that he was reaping the rewards of his investment.

'Now, I'm trying to get my money out and they're saying I can't,' he said to me one morning.

'Dad, what are you doing? You've been duped. This is a scam.'

'No, no scam. It's for real.'

I couldn't convince him otherwise.

When I returned from my next event – at the Surf Ranch in California – I took Dad to see his GP. That was hard: telling the doc about what had been going on as Dad sat next to me, mostly silent but occasionally protesting, 'What? No, I'm fine.'

The doctor did some tests. My father had dementia, he said. How advanced it was, he couldn't be sure.

The next day, I took Dad to hospital for scans. A neurologist sat us down and said my father's illness was a subtype of frontotemporal dementia (FTD) called semantic dementia. A large part of his left temporal lobe had already atrophied, and from this point the disease would most likely progress rapidly.

I'll tell you the basics of this bastard of a disease. It's called semantic dementia because it gradually destroys your semantic memory – everything you have stored by way of words, facts and concepts. You struggle to recall the words for everyday objects, such as television, lamp or motorbike. You might be sitting in a restaurant about to order the lasagne, but when the moment comes, you can't remember the name of the dish you wanted. Your capacity not only to use language but comprehend it diminishes. That's the start and the middle of semantic dementia. It takes away everything you once took for granted: your ability to recognise people, run, walk, shop, care for yourself, stay balanced, resist infection and, eventually, to swallow. Average survival from the time of onset is twelve years.

There was little chance my father would have twelve more years. I found out he'd undergone brain scans five years earlier, in 2014, and kept the diagnosis of early-onset dementia to himself. He had, however, arranged with his solicitor for me to become his legal guardian with power of attorney when he could no longer function.

I thought about our interactions during the last few years. I remembered how slow he was to visit me after Pipe, how I'd needed to spell out for him how rooted I was. I reflected on his visit to Berry that winter, when he'd hammered home a few simple messages. At the time, simplicity was what I'd needed. But had his dementia already robbed him of the ability to perceive the full complexity of my circumstances? Was that what made it possible for him to ignore all the obstacles and see my path forward?

You may have noticed that while I talked about him a lot in the lead-up to Snapper 2017, I've barely mentioned him since until now. The explanation is that, where my dad was concerned, things went quiet. He simply had less to say. Less and less. He was retreating from life. He'd stopped working, giving local kids skateboarding lessons and being active in the community. Although I was still living with him, our conversations had become fewer and shallower, seldom diverging beyond surfing. Even when I'd sought his advice on a topic that had once been a strength of his – property development, say – he'd had little or nothing to say.

Wow, I remember thinking. *I'm on my own here.*

But I hadn't been worried. It didn't occur to me that his issues were medical.

Semantic dementia tends to affect people at a younger age than Alzheimer's disease, with symptoms first appearing in the fifties and sixties. My father received his diagnosis at fifty-seven.

When I heard the prognosis, I went into hyperdrive, researching the entrails out of semantic dementia. It was grim reading. *Currently, there are no known treatments to cure or even slow the progression of FTD . . . it causes progressive and irreversible decline in a person's abilities over a number of years . . . it's a terminal disease.* That's a sample of what I kept banging into. In the realm of complementary medicine, I stumbled across a few ideas, but when I took these to Dad, he was so stuck and uncomprehending that I couldn't get him to go anywhere or see anyone without him getting anxious and defensive. By the start of 2020, it had become too painful and frankly pointless to keep having these confrontations with him.

Reaching out to some of his oldest friends, I had a hard time convincing them that my dad was ill. *That's just Rob*, I kept hearing. *No*, I tried to tell them. I'm not talking about peccadillos here. I'm not talking about idiosyncrasies. I'm talking about the inexorable shutting down of his brain.

As I watched his life crumble, my equilibrium went with it. Every day, I spent hours on the brink of tears. Ever since I could stand, my father had been the central figure in my life. My guide. My rescuer. Many times, through his ability to cut through and inspire with his words, he had taken hold of me as I wobbled, steadying me, and pointing the way forward. I was used to having my dad's peculiar genius to fall back on. I could go wherever I wanted in the world, do whatever

I wanted to do, but if I got hurt or side-tracked I could always come back to him. And now, this insidious disease had stolen his eloquence and robbed of him of the qualities that made him Rob Wright. I kept showing up at events that year, but nothing was working. It felt like my dad was gone, and that I was gone with him.

LIFE DOESN'T STOP, THOUGH. I had a wedding to go to. My own. Kita and I were married on 31 January 2020 at Summergrove Estate – a picturesque venue in Carool in north-eastern New South Wales – which had both lush countryside and ocean views.

'I'd describe the theme and style of our big day as a minimalist, green-and-white midsummer night wedding with elegance,' is some of what Kita told *Vogue* magazine at the time.

Kita was amazing. She refused to be even a faint facsimile of a bridezilla. She took the view that you shouldn't spoil your wedding by succumbing to stress or the desire to control everything; much better to relax and focus on what matters – the fact that you're marrying the person you love in front of everyone you care about. She did make one stipulation on the invitations, however, asking that no one show up in boardshorts. When your guest list includes a horde of surfers, this request was based on a not unrealistic concern.

Kita made sure to honour Tash. In her sister's final hours, Kita had found a patch of paper-daisy bushes in the hospital garden. She picked as many as she could and laid them around Tash's hair and bedside. She later pressed and preserved them as a memento of Tash's last moments on earth. For our wedding, she put some in her bouquet while others were attached to the suits of the groom and groomsmen – best man Keegan, Ty and Stevo, and Tim and Mikey.

It was a happy, beautiful, unforgettable day – all those things – but there was a sad part. I'd wanted my father to speak at my wedding. You know how brides always have something that simply must happen on their wedding day? Well, my dad speaking was my thing.

But as he stood at the microphone, he couldn't speak. He was having a moment because of his condition. It was excruciating for me to watch my strong, proud father struggling in front of everyone. Then his brother, my uncle Ian, and my godfather, Neil Cameron, went to his side and got him going. Dad read his speech haltingly off the page. While it wasn't the multifaceted oration that he would have delivered had he been himself, that was okay because he still gave a speech at my wedding. And I wept through every moment of it.

In the days, weeks and months afterwards, I went into a spin – one of the worst of my spin-laden life. In terms of my surfing, I had a dreadful off-season. I was doing exactly what my father would have frowned on, had he been capable of appraising the situation: training sporadically and drinking too much on weekends.

Then Covid happened and the WSL suspended the tour, so now I'd lost my father and my sport. But that wasn't the end of it. The final component of a triple whammy crash-landed in the middle of 2020, when it became apparent that hundreds of thousands of dollars were missing from my bank accounts. It would be two years before Shane Maree Hatton, who'd been the Wright family bookkeeper for more than a decade and a friend of Mum's, appeared in Wollongong District Court on embezzlement charges. I'll tell you how that played out later.

I was trying to help my dad at home, but his deterioration was accelerating. By mid-2020, he hit a new phase. He stopped being frustrated by his impairments; instead, he became either indifferent or oblivious to them. He appeared to have stopped fighting or caring and just gone blank.

That said, he stuck to his routines. This monstrous thief called dementia was taking everything from him, but it couldn't get its greedy paws on his self-discipline. He couldn't surf anymore, but Dad still rose at dawn every day to exercise; he still took a walk after every meal; and still read (or flicked through) *The Faith I Live By*.

Faith? I was losing faith in myself. Losing faith that I could be like my dad, who never touched alcohol in his life and, as I saw it, never made a mistake except for that business with Mum. Even then, he didn't falter. All he'd needed to do was buckle or fall apart and apologise, but that wasn't his way. He chose to accept the consequences of his decisions.

KITA DIDN'T DESERVE THIS fresh crisis of mine. She'd endured enough already because of me. Although I was at home and spending lots of time with Kita and Vali, I was emotionally unavailable. And Kita was pregnant again: we were expecting our second child in the new year.

Grappling with the loss of my Dad's mind and guidance, my mental health was rapidly declining. In some ways, this was harder to deal with than the head injury. At least with that, I had a plan to adhere to that would eventually make me better. For this, there was no plan of action, no exercises I could do, and I could see that my poor mental health was a threat to not only my marriage but everything that mattered to me.

'I'll get help,' I told Kita. 'I'll fix this.'

In late 2020, I reached out to Jason Patchell – the psychologist I told you about who would help me at the Olympics the following year. I'd been consulting with Jason since 2016, but as Dad's health deteriorated, I needed his help like oxygen.

On 15 January 2021, Kita gave birth to our daughter Rumi. In many ways, it was a rerun of Vali's delivery – another homebirth with the same midwives – though it unfolded more smoothly and quickly for Kita this time. I was surprised by how different it felt to have a daughter than a son. A softer kind of love took root in my heart. As messed up as I was, I suddenly knew this much for certain: I would need to be unfailingly gentle with this sweet little life. It was an exquisite feeling that swept over me at this beautiful time for my family.

At the start of 2021, pro surfing resumed after Covid had scuttled the 2020 tour. I told myself how great this was, how it was just what I needed. But that wasn't how things panned out. If anything, my outlook worsened as the losses piled up and I'd return home from events to find my father in a worse state than when I'd left him.

One day, I made a hopeful but futile attempt to seek my father's counsel on what I should do. I spent a few minutes trying to explain to him how bereft I was and how much I needed his guidance, but it was clear that my words made no sense to him and that I might as well have been spilling my guts to a chair. Dad, it seemed to me, had lost not only his grasp of language but the history of our father–son bond.

The thrust of Jason's advice was that I needed to go easier on myself, to *forgive* myself for failing to meet my dad's standards. No one does life perfectly, he said. Previously, my answer to every life crisis had been discipline and grit, but those qualities weren't going to be much help this time. What I needed was a dose of self-kindness and some hard thinking about how I would lead myself from now on in the absence of my father.

Out of nowhere, I had that momentous result at the Olympics. Secretly, I'd hoped that it would solve everything. It didn't, of course. Because when the cheering stops and the jubilation fades, it's just you again, stuck in your own head. And if you don't know who you are and what to do, there isn't a medal in the world that's going to fix you.

42

OF LATE, LIKE EVERY sport in which concussions happen, surfing has had to work harder at protecting its athletes from brain injury when the financial costs of doing otherwise could be astronomical.

Back in 2015, I reckon most of the world's top sports administrators would have choked on their muesli when they heard that the National Football League in the USA made what's predicted to amount to a $1 billion settlement with thousands of former players, who'd sued over concussions and long-term brain damage. In Australia, where the threat of concussion-related lawsuits hangs heaviest over rugby union, rugby league and Aussie rules, those sports' governing bodies have massively bolstered the rules around concussion management.

For the WSL, my case has been one of numerous spurs to action across the men's and women's tours. In 2019, for example, Courtney Conlogue, a two-time world-title runner-up from California, suffered three concussions in the space of seven months. The third one, which ended her season, occurred in Portugal, where eleven days passed from the time of her knock until she was cleared to fly home.

For 2022, the WSL introduced more stringent protocols around head injuries, requiring a surfer who's suffered a concussion to return to their pre-injury baseline of cognitive functioning (established in pre-season testing) before they're allowed to compete again. The rationale is that if you return to competition prematurely and suffer another brain injury before you've fully healed, the effects can be cumulative, and you risk serious and possibly permanent brain damage.

While I can't say for sure that I entered the surf on that fateful morning at Pipeline carrying the lingering effects of an earlier concussion, I do think it's possible. I also have to say that if I didn't take an appalling risk that day, then I've almost certainly taken just such risks at other, earlier times in my life when I didn't know any better. Raised in a different era by an old-school father, I was taught to be tough rather than prudent.

At the start of 2022, the WSL announced it would make helmets available to all competitors at the big-wave venues of Pipeline and Teahupo'o. As things stand, no surfer is required to use a helmet in competition – just as no international cricketer is obliged to wear a helmet when facing the world's fastest bowlers – but it's there if you want it. I suspect it won't be long before the surfing helmet becomes as ubiquitous as its cricketing equivalent. My experience is that once you've worn protective headgear in a pumping surf, you soon feel naked without it.

In the wake of my TBI, I have never crusaded for the mandatory use of helmets in pro surfing or the toughening of WSL protocols. Frankly, I've been preoccupied with getting healthy, competing, being a husband and father – and caring for my ailing father. Also, I don't think I need to be a crusader.

The facts of what happened to me, combined with the push for change happening across sport generally, have been more than enough for the WSL to wake up and act on concussion in its ranks.

What I have done, however, is respond to the hundreds of people who've reached out to me on social media about my recovery. In most cases, these people – not necessarily surfers – had suffered serious concussions and were struggling. Some wanted my advice, others thanked me for inspiring them – for giving them hope that there's a way back for them. Let me tell you, many of those people who reached out inspired me, too.

IN THE CONTEXT OF past head injuries, I need to say something about both my father's dementia and my heightened risk or otherwise of developing a degenerative brain condition.

Dad's been a fanatical surfer all his life. As you'd appreciate by now, he was also someone who was wired to absorb his knocks and keep moving forward. While he never suffered a head injury as serious as mine, I know that as a hard-charging surfer he would have taken his share of hits over the years, and that he'd have brushed these off as trivial. That's Dad. A lot of the photos on the walls in his house show him riding fifteen-foot waves.

I can't say for sure whether past head knocks played a role in my dad's dementia. I'm not sure anyone can. But I did read a 2021 study by the Perelman School of Medicine at the University of Pennsylvania that showed a single head injury could lead to dementia later in life. Compared to participants who'd never had a concussion, a single concussion was associated with a 1.25 times increased risk of dementia. When there were two or more head injuries, the risk doubled.

Keep in mind that even a doubled risk of dementia doesn't make you all that likely to get it. From my reading of the data, a history of two or more concussions would increase your chances of getting dementia by the age of sixty-five from 1 in 50 to 1 in 25.

As for my longer-term prospects, another potential boogey man is chronic traumatic encephalopathy (CTE), a degenerative brain disease found in people – often athletes and military personnel – with a history of brain trauma. CTE used to be known as dementia pugilistica or punch-drunk syndrome, because doctors suspected it was confined to boxers. But we know now that it's not. Here's what else I've found out about CTE.

Its first symptoms tend to appear in a person's forties – years or even decades after they've recovered from their last concussion, or stopped receiving relatively minor but repetitive head knocks. It seems you don't need to have sustained a single concussion to develop CTE. It's enough to have taken a lot of what doctors call sub-concussive knocks over a period of years. Whether you have a history of concussion or a history of these minor knocks, you're at a higher risk of CTE than someone whose sport was, say, tennis or golf. Across the severity spectrum, head knocks can trigger irreversible changes in the brain, specifically the build-up of a protein called tau. (Tau: it sounds innocent enough, like a form of meditation or a martial arts practice, but it's a leading culprit in CTE.)

The first symptoms of CTE tend to be headaches and problems with concentration. Memory loss, mood swings and impulse-control issues come later. Eventually, CTE develops into full-blown dementia, and sufferers typically die within ten years of symptom onset from respiratory failure, heart disease, suicide or problems associated with end-stage dementia. It's only after death that a definitive CTE diagnosis can be made.

There's still a lot that doctors don't know about CTE – for instance, why some people get it and most people don't. I've had a bunch of concussions and a TBI, but that doesn't mean I'm going to develop CTE, whereas some guy who stopped playing rugby when he finished school – and never suffered a concussion – might. There's no magic number of hits, severe or otherwise, that applies here. Some degree of genetic pre-disposition must come into play. It's also possible that the stage of life at which the head knocks occur is important. Just as sun damage incurred in childhood seems to put you at a higher risk of developing skin cancer in your lifetime than sun damage incurred in adulthood, something similar might apply to head knocks and CTE.

In the first half of 2022, I asked myself: *Will I be okay?* There are no guarantees, but are there ever? About anything? When it comes to brain health, fate dealt my family a challenging hand. Between my mother, my father and me, we've kept various neurosurgeons, neurologists and sundry other brain experts busy. I figure all I can do is take care of myself and hope for the best.

EPILOGUE

Kita, Vali, Rumi and I still live with my dad in his house at Lennox Head. I've struggled to let go. He needs me and I keep a close eye on him whenever I'm around.

He has a carer who comes every day to help him with shopping and food preparation. He doesn't understand or say much, but he knows who I am – at times. His wish is to stay in his house for as long as possible, and I'll see that he does.

The doctors have nothing to offer. Their medicine bags are empty. For a while, they prescribed drugs that helped to subdue Dad's frustration and emotional breakdowns, but they aren't needed anymore because the frustration and breakdowns are no more; they've been replaced by this awful emptiness.

Leading into the 2022 tour, I was still suffering from mild concussion-like symptoms from a small knock and feeling like shit from that already, never mind the guilt of leaving my family and father behind. I booked a flight to Hawaii for the first event – and didn't show up at the airport. I booked another flight – and missed that one, too. I was lost, which is how I'd felt to varying degrees since my dad started losing his mind.

In the end, I decided I couldn't just leave the tour by disappearing, so I showed up at Pipeline. Paddling out, though, even in this place that had once seemed mythical, I was asking myself: *What am I doing here?* With an attitude like that, you can't expect to succeed. I couldn't get much happening at most stops and eventually failed to make the midseason cut by one position. Despite my effort dig deep and find that grit again, the world had other plans: I was off the tour.

Life wasn't easy after that, as it threw me some tough news about my brain, but I made some changes for the good. Fresh off the tour, I felt compelled to take the family to Uluwatu, Indonesia. It felt like it was calling me again. Tyler and her now-wife Lily came, too. It was so special to be able to share our memories of Dad in his favourite place in the world. It was the perfect way to unwind from the stress of the tour and the first time I had found some peace of mind about my father's condition. I feel I've gained strength from prioritising my mental health and being honest with people about how I'm really going. And all of this – this campaign to be a better man – might just be what I look back on most proudly.

In June 2022, I consulted Professor Charlie Teo, the neurosurgeon who'd operated on my mother in 2016, for a fresh assessment of my condition. I saw him in Sydney at Cingulum Health, where he's the medical director and co-founder.

Charlie reviewed my case, conducted various tests, and questioned me about my injuries and symptoms, past and present. He told me that, considering the number and severity of head knocks I'd sustained, he was concerned about my long-term health. Any knock I suffered from now on, he warned, would be hard to recover from.

'For now, I can fix you and make you feel better,' he said. 'But if you get more head knocks, you'll end up with early-onset dementia.'

As can often be the case with medical opinions on complex conditions, Charlie's warning contrasted with the advice I'd received from Paul. While it would have been easy to feel confused, my inclination was to heed my gut reaction – and my gut reaction was to start prioritising other elements of my life besides surfing. For her part, Kita was rattled by Charlie's words and wanted me to retire from surfing immediately – no swansongs, no last hurrahs.

But when you've been surfing since you could walk, when you've loved it and needed it as I have, you don't walk away easily. You can't help but wonder what might still be possible.

I wasn't going to quit just like that. Instead, I flew to Melbourne to see Brett and received several days' treatment from him.

'Let's get you feeling right first and then you can make a decision,' Brett said.

As it happened, fate dangled a carrot in front of my nose: the idea of finishing my career at the Olympics. The host city for the 2024 Games is Paris, but the venue for the surfing is my happy hunting ground of Teahupo'o, Tahiti. In 2022, Surfing Australia learned it may be eligible to send a third male surfer to the Games – a kind of wildcard pick. They advised me that I was in contention for that spot and that I should 'stay relevant'. Of course, my interest was piqued, and I accepted an invitation from Surfing Australia to attend the tour event at Teahupo'o in August.

Shortly before I left, I returned to Cingulum for a week of treatment that included something called transcranial magnetic stimulation, which helped with my cognitive functioning and ability to multitask. I also had the chance to speak with Charlie again about the advice he'd given me and the lure of another Olympics.

'Are you serious about what you said?' I asked him.

'I am *a hundred per cent* serious,' he replied.

'Because I want to let you know that what you said has impacted me massively. I've been really struggling with energy and motivation, with what to do with my life, since you told me that. You see, you might tell someone else the same thing, but they've never seen what dementia looks like. I know what it looks like. I've seen how ugly it is because my dad's got it.'

Charlie's response was to look me hard in the eyes. 'Good,' he said. 'You know what it looks like. You know what you'll be in for. You know what decision to make.'

Wow, I thought, *this guy's straight down the line. He's not being flippant about my career. He's factored in surfing's place in my life and he's adamant I should walk away.*

Still, I persisted. 'But if I get another head knock, I can come back here and get more treatment, right?'

'Look, I can make you feel better,' Charlie said. 'But I can't replace brain matter. And that's what you're going to struggle with later on.'

I felt my eyes narrow. 'I thought you were a risk-taker.'

'No, not with this. You don't want to mess with this.'

Only a couple of months after this exchange, Charlie made the news for all the wrong reasons. *The Sydney Morning Herald, The Age* and *60 Minutes* ran stories accusing him of charging large sums to perform futile operations that catastrophically injured two child patients. Charlie has consistently denied any legal, professional or ethical wrong-doing.

There's no point my delving into the specifics of those cases, which are achingly sad. As a father, I can imagine the agony of seeing your child struck down by something as dreadful as a brain tumour. I can imagine pinning your hopes for a cure on an operation performed by one of the country's leading neurosurgeons. And I can imagine the devastation that would overwhelm you when that operation fails. My heart bleeds for the parents of those two children.

But here's my perspective on Charlie, who's operated on not only my mother but quite a few people I know, including friends and friends' parents. I see Charlie as a man who saves lives. This is what I've heard from more people than I can count: 'Charlie Teo saved my life.' As a surgeon, has he ever made a mistake? I don't expect he'd be human if he hadn't. Has he ever taken on an operation that was more than likely doomed to failure? Most likely. But I can't condemn him for those choices. And my impression is that for every one patient who's had a poor outcome under Charlie, there are a hundred who've been cured. As for his dealings with me, there was no trace of the maverick or gung-ho neurosurgeon that his critics paint him as. His advice could not have been more conservative. Quit now. Protect your brain. Stop taking risks.

'You might not like the message,' he said. 'But you need to be informed. You need to hear this.'

With Charlie's words echoing in my ears, I went to Tahiti. There, my course became clear. On my first morning, I looked out on a pounding Teahupo'o swell and thought, *Nope, I don't want any part of this.* I love the wave there and I'd love to get more big barrels, but to do well at Teahupo'o you need to take risks, you need to take wipeouts in practice, and I knew I wasn't prepared to do those things anymore. The trip became a chance for me to say goodbye to that wave, to put its perils and possibilities behind me. More than just Teahupo'o and the Olympics, I was resolved to walk away from competition surfing altogether. With that came a blend of great sadness and a crazy kind of joy and relief. After years of clinging to my sport, which was sustaining me on one level but threatening everything I cherished on another, I'd finally let go.

Today, eight months on from that decision, I feel happier and healthier than I have for a long time. My brain is in good shape – and I'd like to keep it that way. That said, I couldn't resist a swansong. I wanted to compete in one last event, and the one I chose was Bells Beach at Easter 2023. I took a wildcard to get in so I could say goodbye to competitive surfing on a manageable wave.

And Bells was everything it could have been.

Predictably, I fell ill in the lead-up, wracked by fevers, splitting headaches and fatigue. But none of it discouraged me because, hell, what was new? By this stage I was so accustomed to overcoming the protests of my own body that getting crook before my final event felt almost appropriate.

About a month before Bells, I'd relinked with my friend and former coach Micro, keen to tap his knack for simplifying the objectives of competitive surfing. This felt like the perfect time to revive the spirit of Snapper 2017. You know, just take off and stay on my board. Me against the water, man. For my final event, I wanted surfing to be as pure and uncomplicated as that.

I won my first heat, which featured Filipe Toledo, the reigning world champion. Surfing felt easy. I was red hot. Shortly before my next heat, I spent a few minutes with Jason Patchell.

'No matter what happens today,' I said, 'I'm ready for this to be over. All the resilience I've had to develop, all the character-building shit I've been through, it's all been worth it, but now it's time to listen to my body.' And with that I started to cry. From sadness? No. From relief and satisfaction and the sense of an ending.

I paddled out and nailed my waves but was pipped by Ethan Ewing, who went on to win the event. My feet had barely touched the sand when my two of my oldest buddies, Ty and Keegan, hoisted me onto their shoulders and chaired me up the beach as my extended family surrounded us and my fellow surfers cheered. It was as though I was being carried from one life to the next.

Earlier, my family received justice with regards to Shane Maree Hatton, who'd betrayed our trust and friendship by stealing from us over the course of a decade. In July 2022, in the Wollongong District Court, she was sentenced to five years and six months in prison for embezzling more than $1.5 million from Tyler and me, as well as smaller sums from Mum, Dad and

Mikey. As well as incarceration, the judge ordered her to pay us compensation totalling more than $500,000.

Where to from here? I'm not exactly sure, but I know who I am and the strength I have inside. I feel I have the confidence to go anywhere. I'd like to stay involved in surfing, ideally as a coach or mentor to the next generation of Australia's most promising surfers. After more than a decade on the tour and with everything I've been through, I know I could help them fulfil their potential. From where I'm standing, I see Ethan Ewing and Jack Robinson as two young guys equipped to win world titles one day. On my last trip to Tahiti, I had the pleasure of working with Ethan, whose dad was with him just as my dad had been alongside me when I was starting out.

Pro surfing tests every aspect of your character. So does life, which can hit like a truck. To make it work, you need people, good people, people you love and who love you back, at your side. Don't try to do life on your own. Take it on, absolutely. But take it on with people in your corner.

ABOUT THE AUTHOR

IN 2015, AUSSIE SURFING legend Owen Wright was on the brink of a world title only to have his hopes dashed when he suffered a serious brain injury ahead of the final for the Pipeline Masters competition in Hawaii. In a single moment, he went from being ranked fifth in the world in surfing to having to learn how to walk and talk again. However, in 2017, Owen returned to form, immediately claiming victory at the opening event of the Champions Tour, part of a winning streak that has seen him most recently awarded the bronze medal for surfing at the Tokyo Olympics. His sister, Tyler Wright, is also a world champion surfer. Owen lives with his wife Kita Alexander and their children at Lennox Head, on the northern coast of New South Wales.

Find out more about Owen via Instagram (@owright) or Facebook (www.facebook.com/RealOwenWright).